入るかな？ はみ出ちゃった。
～宮本佳明 建築団地
2023年9月16日(土)−10月22日(日)

[開館時間]10:00～18:00(ただし入場は17:30まで)
[主催]宝塚市立文化芸術センター(指定管理者:宝塚みらい創造ファクトリー)
[協賛]総合資格学院, 株式会社東畑建築事務所, 株式会社ナカミツ建工, 兵庫ベンダ工業株式会社
[協力]株式会社フリックスタジオ [後援]神戸新聞社

宮本佳明 建築

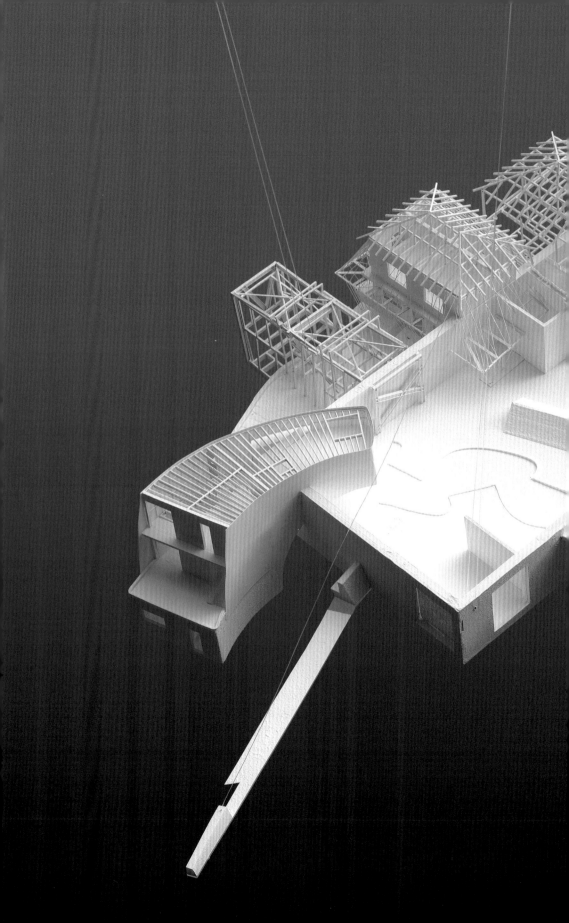

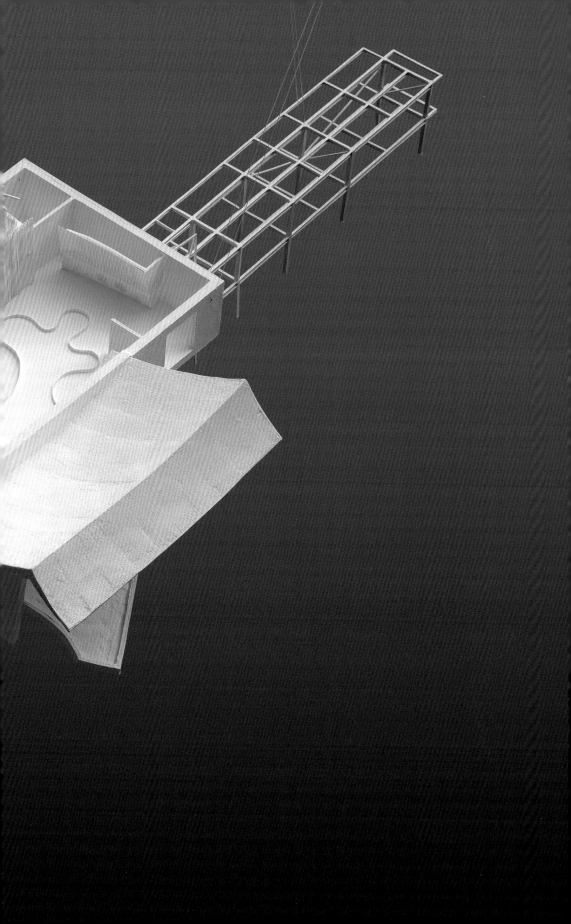

ushin-ji Temple
est's Quarters

est's Quarters

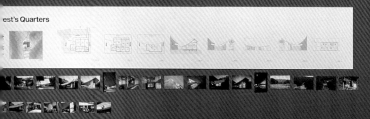

Korin-ji Temple Façade R

Korin-ji Temple Façade Renovation

入るかな？はみ出ちゃった。〜宮本佳明 建築団地

Full Size is oversized: KATSUHIRO MIYAMOTO Architecture Park

会期：2023年9月16日（土）〜10月22日（日）
会場：宝塚市立文化芸術センター2F メインギャラリー（宝塚市武庫川町7-64）
主催：宝塚市立文化芸術センター
原寸大模型製作・インストール：株式会社ゴードー
グラフィックデザイン：佐藤大介［sato design.］

協賛：総合資格学院／株式会社東畑建築事務所／公益財団法人戸田育英財団／
株式会社ナカミツ建工／兵庫ベンダ工業株式会社
協力：早稲田大学宮本佳明研究室／株式会社フリックスタジオ
後援：神戸新聞社

受賞：令和5年度（第74回）文化庁芸術選奨
文部科学大臣賞（美術B部門）

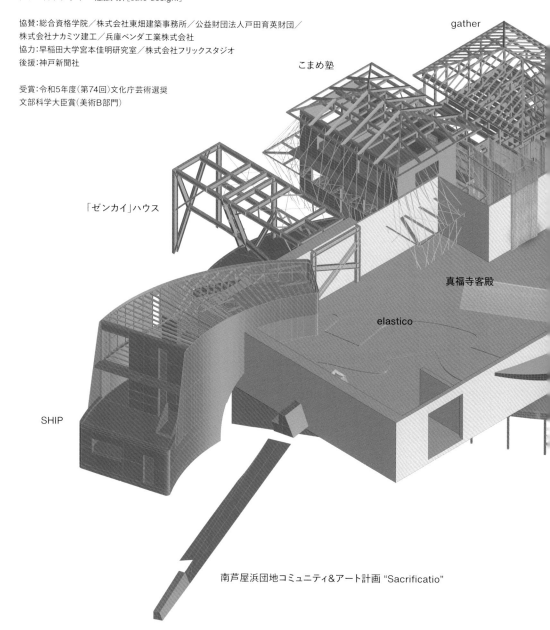

gather

こまめ塾

「ゼンカイ」ハウス

真福寺客殿

elastico

SHIP

南芦屋浜団地コミュニティ＆アート計画 "Sacrificatio"

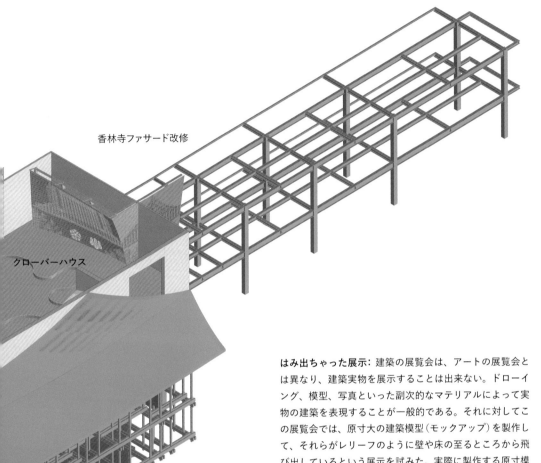

香林寺ファサード改修

クローバーハウス

澄心寺庫裏

はみ出ちゃった展示： 建築の展覧会は、アートの展覧会とは異なり、建築実物を展示することは出来ない。ドローイング、模型、写真といった副次的なマテリアルによって実物の建築を表現することが一般的である。それに対してこの展覧会では、原寸大の建築模型（モックアップ）を製作して、それらがレリーフのように壁や床の至るところから飛び出しているという展示を試みた。実際に製作する原寸模型は建築物の一部分に過ぎないが、鑑賞者の想像力を借りることによって、壁や床の向こう側に建築空間の全体像を浮かび上がらせることが出来るのではないかと考えた。いわば展示室（ホワイトキューブ）からはみ出ちゃった展示である。多様な用途の建築物が展示室という一つの「敷地」に会して建つことから、「建築団地」と名付けている。

Exhibition out of bounds: Unlike art exhibitions, it is impossible to display actual architectural works in architectural exhibitions. In most cases, the actual architecture is represented by secondary materials such as drawings, models, and photographs. In this exhibition, on the other hand, full-scale architectural models (mock-ups) were made and displayed as if they were reliefs, emerging from the walls and floors. Even though the actual full-scale models form only a part of the architecture, I thought that by borrowing the viewer's imagination, it would be possible to create an overall image of the architectural space beyond the walls and floors. In other words, it is an exhibition that has strayed outside the exhibition room (so-called "white cube"). The name 'Architecture Park' is derived from the fact that buildings of various functions are gathered on a single "site," the exhibition room.

宮本佳明建築団地

KATSUHIRO MIYAMOTO
Architecture Park

Contents

KATSUHIRO MIYAMOTO &
Works: 1992−

この作品集は、2023年秋に開催した展覧会をきっかけにして編集したものです。図録という意味も込めて、巻頭には展覧会のドキュメントを配しました。本編は展示作品も含め、これまでの設計活動の中から、完成に至った建築やアートを中心に約30作品を選んで構成しています。展覧会と同じく「建築団地」と名付けたタイトルが示す通り、住宅、寺院、美容室、医院、学校など、さまざまな用途の建築が並んでいます。繚乱の建築群がつくる街並の散歩を、心ゆくまで楽しんでください。（宮本佳明）

ASSOCIATES

This collection of works was compiled as a wrap-up to an exhibition held in the fall of 2023. In order to serve as a catalog, we have included documentation of the exhibition at the beginning of the book. The main volume is composed of about 30 works including the exhibited works, which focus on completed architecture and art projects selected from design activities to date. As the exhibition title, "Architecture Park," suggests, the works include a variety of building types, such as houses, temples, beauty salon, clinic, school, etc. Please enjoy to your heart's content, a walk through the townscape created by the blooming architecture. (Katsuhiro Miyamoto)

子どもだけが
そのまま飛び込んでこられる
跳ね上げ戸。

The flip-up doors that only children could jump through.

Open-Air Kindergarten
1992

幼稚園の図書室と遊戯室を兼ねた小さな建築である。園庭の端に位置する敷地は、川に向かって岬状に張り出し、背後からは隣地の雑木林が覆いかぶさる。園庭に置かれた他の遊具と同じように、この建築自体が子どもたちにとって遊具と感じられるようにデザインを考えた。ガススプリングによって柔らかく持ち上げられた跳ね上げ戸は、開放状態がデフォルトであり、子どもたちだけが園庭から飛び込んでこられるように高さを設定している。跳ね上げ戸は片持ち屋根と共に全体として大きなキャノピーを形成する。キャノピーの下では、座り込んで絵本を読んでいる子どもの傍らを他の子どもが園庭の延長のように走り抜けていく。一方で、母の会や編み物教室といったよりプライベートな集まりに対応したスペースは、古い石積みの擁壁を正確にカットして、そこに嵌め込むように地階に置いている。地上とは対照的に、雑木林からの木漏れ日に包まれる落ち着いた空間である。

This is a small building that also serves as a library and play-room for a kindergarten. Located at the edge of the kinder-garten yard, the site juts out like a promontory towards the river, while a wooded area on neighboring land covers it from behind. The design was conceived so that the building itself would feel like one of the many playground equipment in the kindergarten yard for the children. The flip-up doors lifted gently with gas springs, default to the open position and are set at a height that allows children only to jump in and out from the yard. The flip-up doors, together with the cantile-vered roof, form a large canopy as a whole. Some children could run past a child who is sitting and reading a picture book, all under the canopy as if it were an extension of the kindergarten yard. On the other hand, a space for more pri-vate gatherings such as mothers' meetings or knitting class-es is placed at the basement level where it appears to fit in a precisely cut-out old masonry retaining wall. In contrast to the ground level, this is a calm space enveloped in sunlight filtering through the trees from the wooded area.

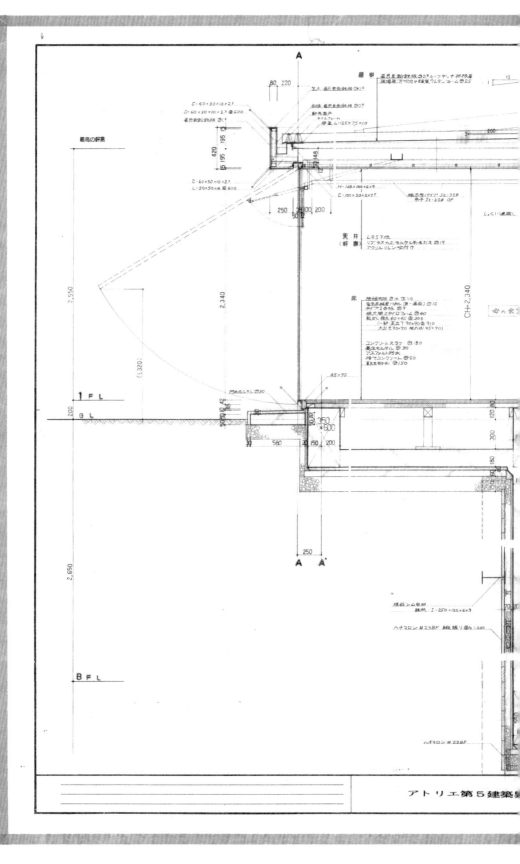

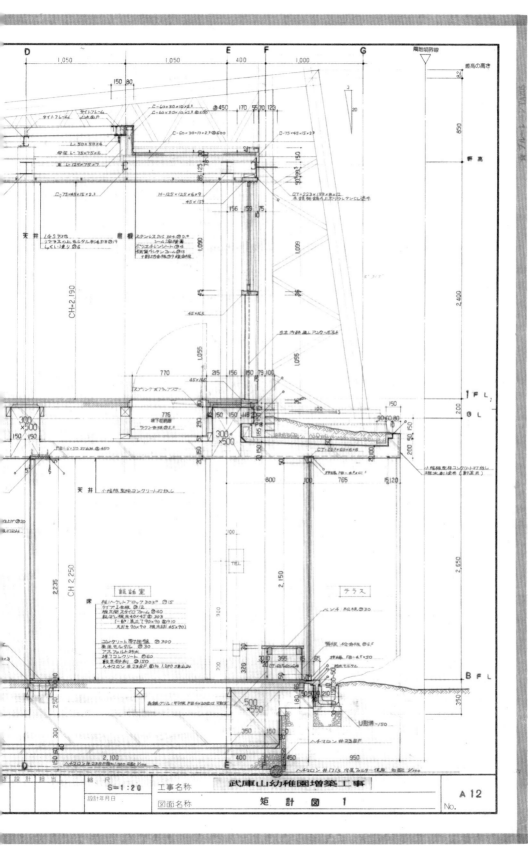

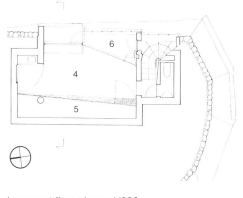

basement floor plan s=1/200

1 playroom	4 mother's club
2 porch	5 storage
3 open veranda	6 light court

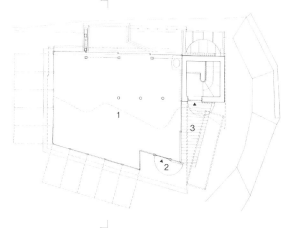

1st floor plan s=1/200

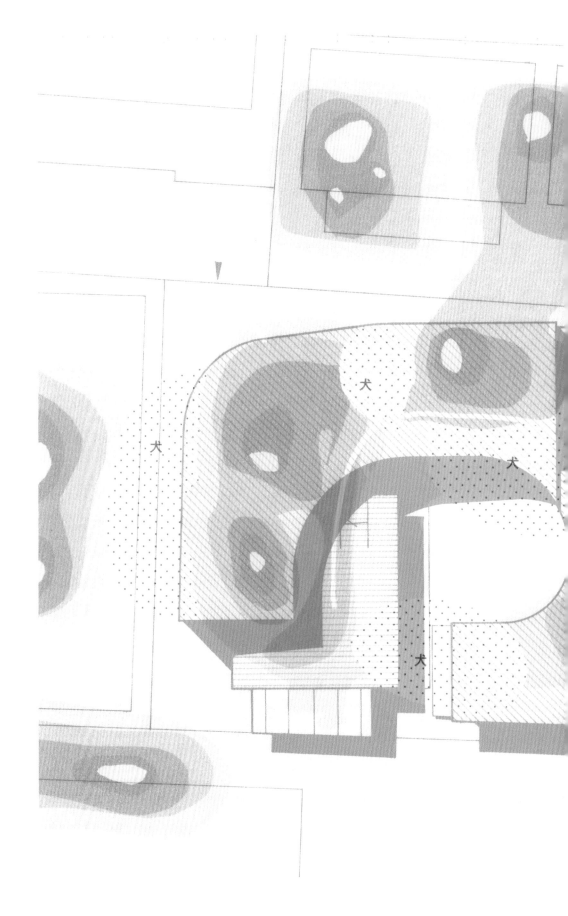

犬

しなやかで連続的な、
社会をも連環していけるような
居住システム。

A flexible, continuous, and even socially interconnected
residential system.

家族文化アパートメント「愛田荘」
AIDA-SOU: Apartment House for Family

1995

この「住宅」には、母親と、娘2人、男女の居候の計6人、
加えて犬6匹からなる拡大家族が雑居的に住まう。中庭の
周りを巡るスロープに各自の〈部屋〉が木賃アパートのよ
うに取り付くが、ここでいう〈部屋〉はユニットと呼びうる
ような完結的なものではない。住人の成熟度に応じて、共
用あるいは専用のキチネット、シャワーなどが適宜設けら
れており、それらが集まって〈家〉と呼ぶルースな3つのエ
リアを構成する。〈部屋〉同士は相互補完的であり、住人は
必要に応じてスロープや、土間、縁を介して、訪問型の選
択的コミュニケーションを展開することになる。このプロ
ジェクトはリジッドな「個室群住居」をモデルとしたもので
はない。むしろ逆のベクトル、すなわちすでに解体の完了
した個のスムーズな再契約を促すような装置系をイメージ
している。ルースにルースに、しなやかで連続的な、さら
には社会をも連環していけるような、そんな居住システム
を夢見ている。

This "residence" houses an extended family consisting of a
mother, two daughters, a male and female housemate, and
six dogs. Each "room" is attached to the ramp around the
courtyard in the manner of a Japanese-style lodging house
called *mokuchin apart(ment)*, but the "room" here is not a
complete unit. Depending on the degree of independence of
the residents, shared or private kitchenettes, showers, and so
forth are provided as needed. All of these are gathered and
configured into three loose areas known as "houses." The
"rooms" are complementary to each other, and residents are
encouraged to visit and selectively communicate with each
other via the ramp, the earthen floor, and the veranda at the
edge of the house as needed. This project is not modeled on
the formal conception of "individual living units." Rather, it is
a move in the opposite direction, which is a mechanism that
will facilitate the smooth re-contracting of already atomized
individuals. I envision a loose, flexible, continuous, and even
socially interconnected residential system.

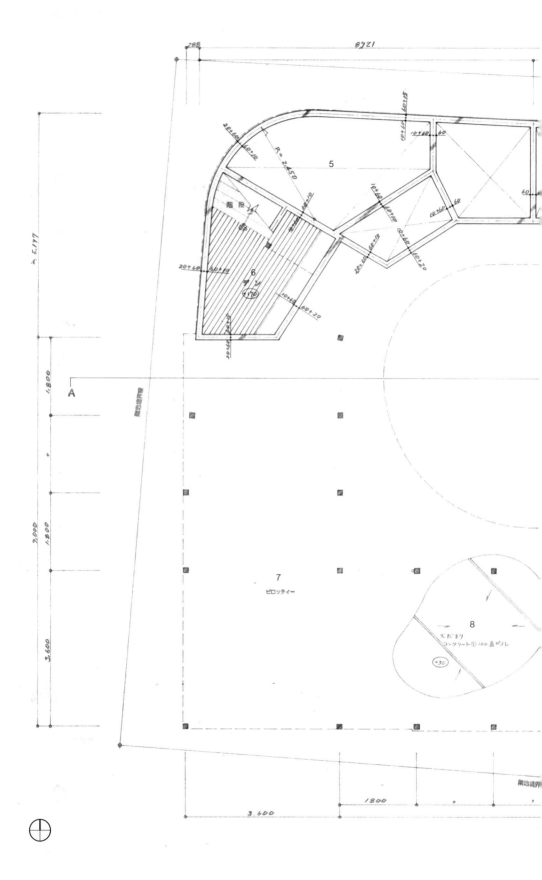

平 面 図

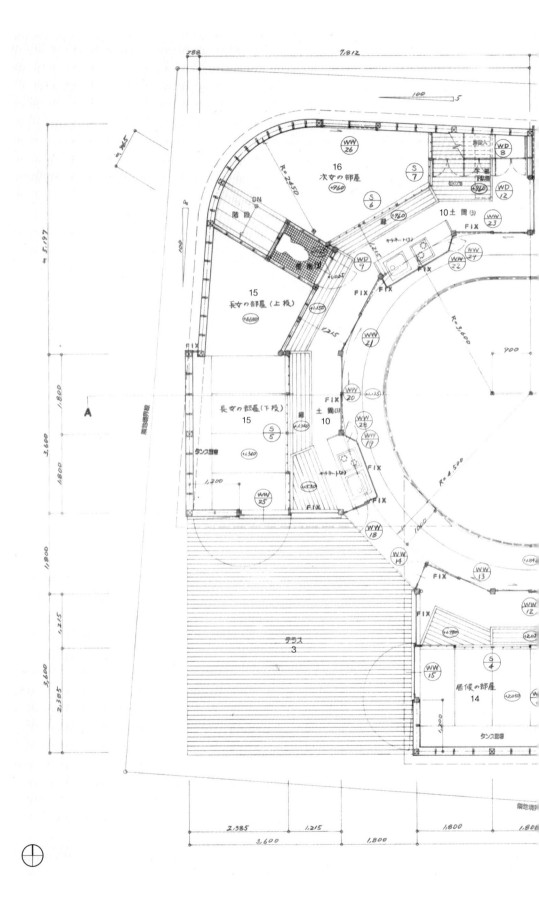

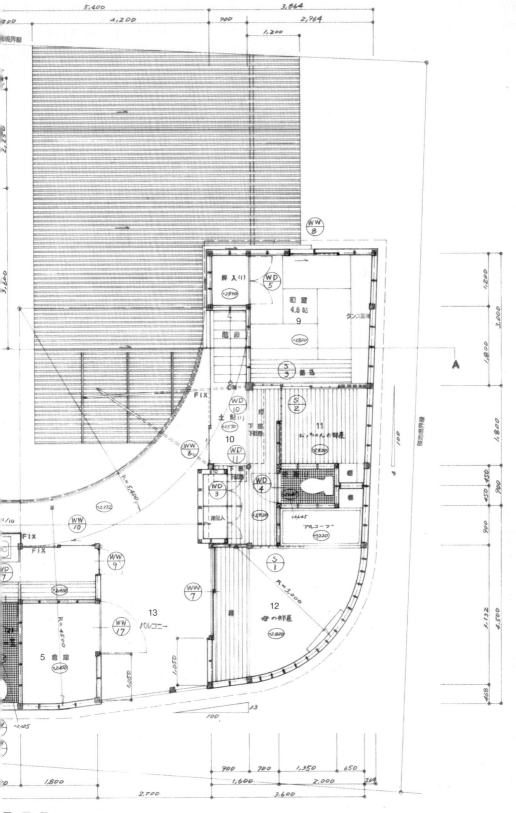

平 面 図

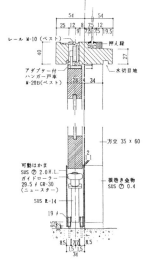

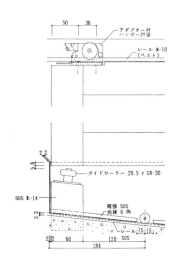

glass sliding door skirting detail s=1/7

1 dining room
2 porch
3 terrace
4 court
5 storage
6 den
7 pilotis
8 space for dogs
9 tatami room
10 earthen floor
11 "Companion's" room
12 mother's room
13 balcony
14 friend's room
15 elder daughter's room
16 second daughter's room

south-north section s=1/200

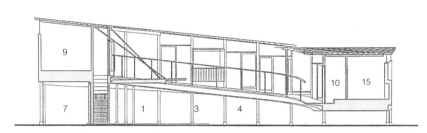

east-west section s=1/200

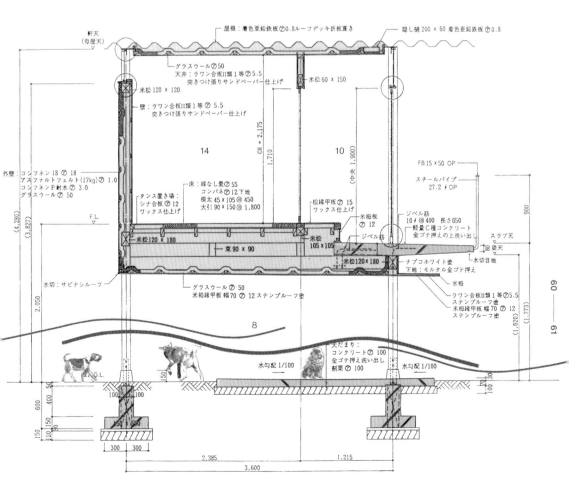

sectional detail s=1/50

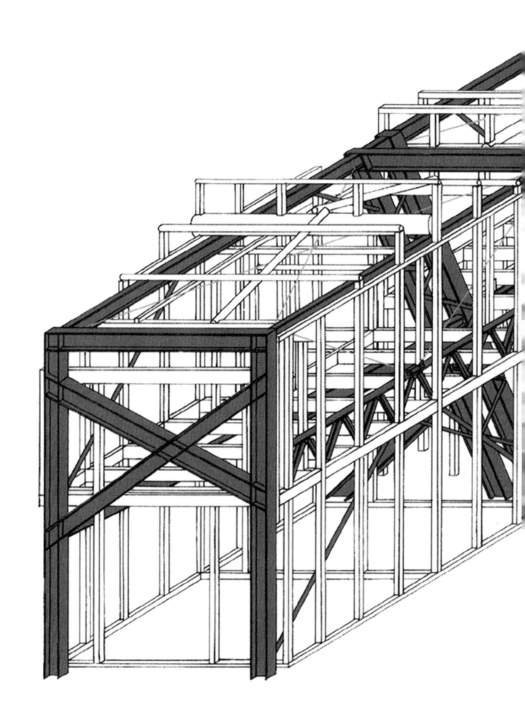

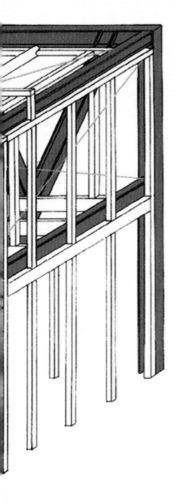

ウルトラ耐震補強。
──公費解体制度への異議申し立て。

Ultra seismic reinforcement.
──A challenge to the Publicly Funded Demolition System.

「ゼンカイ」ハウス
House Surgery ("ZENKAI" HOUSE)
1997

阪神淡路大震災で全壊判定を受けた築110年の自宅長屋の修復プロジェクトである。震災後広く利用された公費解体制度は、公費修繕というオルタナティブが同時に用意されなかったために、事実上の解体指導として機能したことは否定できない。このプロジェクトは、「全壊」の判定が半ば自動的に公費解体を意味したという構図に対して、実際の修復計画を通じて異議申し立てを行ったものである。既存の傷んだ木造軸組はそのままに、そこに新たな鉄骨の構造体を併置して耐震性の向上を図った。生活の支障にならないスペースを選んで鉄骨を通し、木造軸組を随所で安定した新しい鉄骨フレームに緊結する。将来的には木造の荷重は徐々に鉄骨に預け替えられてゆく。木造軸組はいずれ構造体としての役目を終え、住まい手と震災の記憶を留めた造作となって生き続けることになる。たとえ文化財的価値を持つものでなくとも、建築は常に「記憶の器」としての側面を持っている。

This project is a restoration of a 110-year-old row house that was judged "completely collapsed" after the Great Hanshin-Awaji Earthquake. A system of publicly funded demolition widely used after the earthquake functioned as de facto "demolition guidance" because the alternative of publicly funded renovation was not provided at the same time. Through an actual restoration plan, this project challenges the assumption that a judgement of "completely collapsed" means semi-automatically that demolition at public expense is warranted. The existing damaged wooden framework was left intact, and a new steel frame structure was placed alongside it to improve earthquake resistance. The wooden frame was connected to the new stable steel frame at various points, with the steel frame passing through selected spaces where it would not interfere with daily life. I suppose that the loads will be gradually transferred to the steel framework in the future. The wooden framework will eventually cease to function as a structure, and it will remain as a feature that preserves the memory of residents and of the earthquake. Architecture always has an aspect of being a "vessel of memory," even if it has no cultural value.

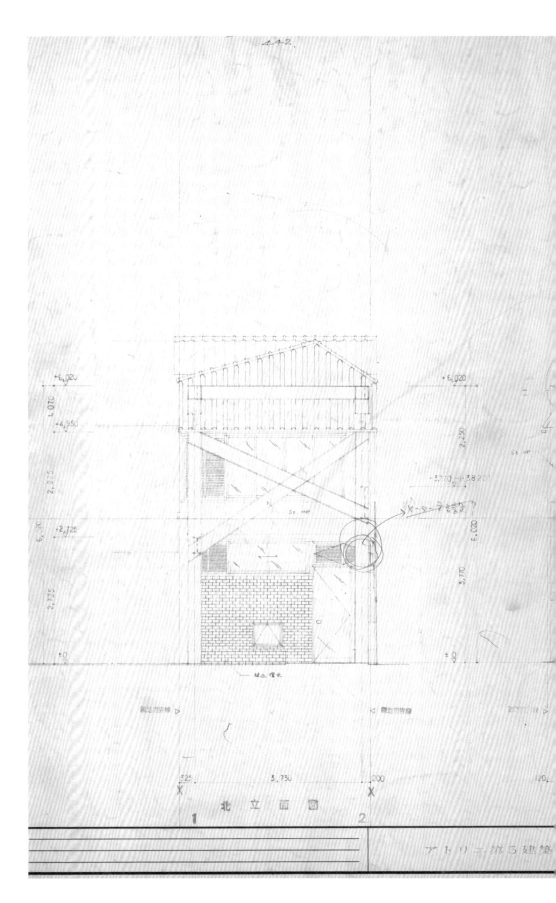

北 立 面 図

アトリエ棟 5 建築

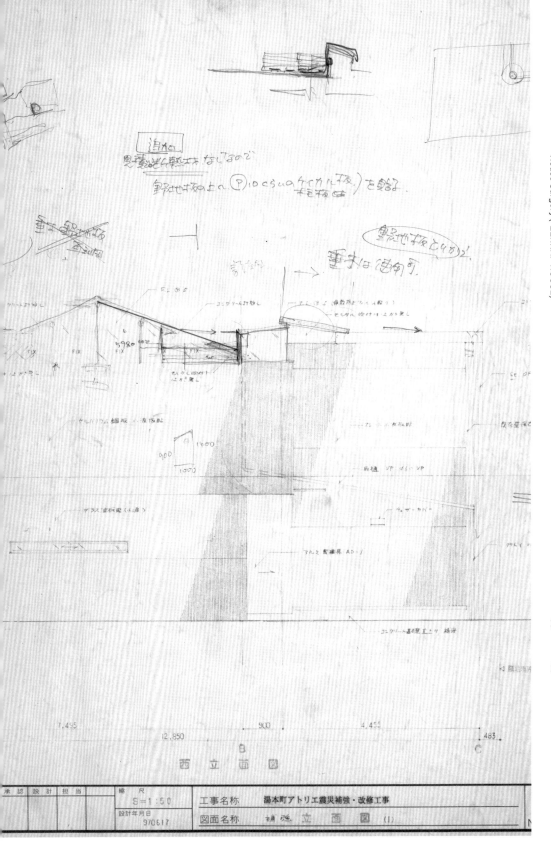

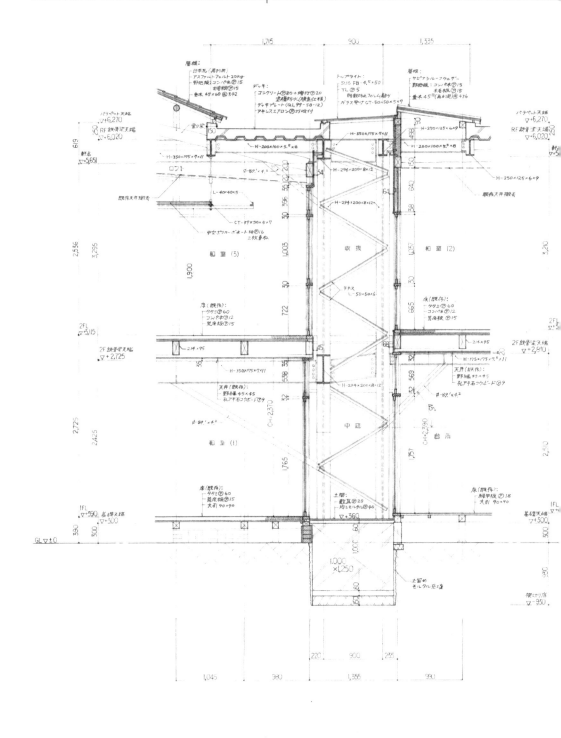

屋根：
日本瓦(高がわ用)
アスファルトフェルト 20kg
野地板 コンパネ⑦15
衣青板⑦15
垂木 45×60 @ 342

デッキ：
コンクリート⑦80+増打⑦20
塗膜防水(開長仕様)
デッキプレート(QLデク-50-12)
アキレスエアロン⑦25吹付

トップライト：
SUS FB-4.5×50
TL⑦5
耐動防火フィルム貼り
ガラス受けGT-50×50×5×7

屋根：
サビナラルーフウェザー
野地板 コンパネ⑦15
木垂木⑦15
垂木 45□(高50剛)@436

パラペット天端
▽+6,270
250 RF鉄骨梁天端
▽+6,020

軒高
▽+5,651

パラペット天端
▽+6,270
RF鉄骨梁天端
▽+6,020

H-350×175×7×11

ロント

φ-89ブレース

L-40×40×5

既存天井撤去

CT-89×50×6×7
中空ポリカーボネート板⑦16
2枚重ね

和室 (5)

吹抜

和室 (2)

H-200×100×5.5×8

H-350×175×7×11

H-294×200×8×12

H-250×125×6×9

H-200×100×5.5×8

H-250×125×6×9

既存天井撤去

ラチス
L-50×50×6

床 (既存)：
タタミ⑦60
コンパネ⑦12
荒床板⑦15

床 (既存)：
タタミ⑦60
コンパネ⑦12
荒床板⑦15

2FL
▽+3,115

2F鉄骨梁天端
▽+2,725

2F鉄骨梁天端
▽+2,810

2-14×95

2-14×95

H-350×175×7×11

H-175×175×7×11

天井 (既存)：
野緑縁 45×45
礼アト石コウボード⑦9

天井 (既存)：
野縁縁 45×45
礼アト石コウボード⑦9

H-294×200×8×12

φ-89ブレース×4.2

φ-89ブレース×4.2

CH-2,370

CH-2,370

和室 (1)

中庭

台所

床 (既存)：
タタミ⑦60
荒床板⑦15
大引 90×90

土間：
敷瓦⑦29
均モルタル⑦40
▽+360

床 (既存)：
耐水板⑦18
大引 90×90

1FL
▽+590 基礎葉天端
▽+300

1FL
▽+500

GL▽±0

1,000
×1,250

土留め
モルタル充填

根切り底
▽-350

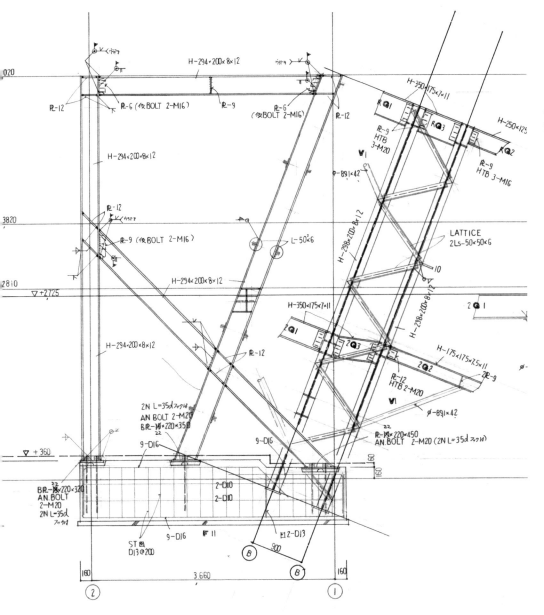

(B)(B') FRAME 鉄骨詳細図 1/30

現場溶接卸合の フランヂ卸合は銅板裏当しスカラッフ゜
ウェフ゛卸合は仮ボールト撤去後穴埋め

工場1回, 現場建方後補修塗

アトリエ第5建築界

承認	設計	担当		略 尺

設計年月日
97

one year after the Hanshin-Awaji Great Earthquake

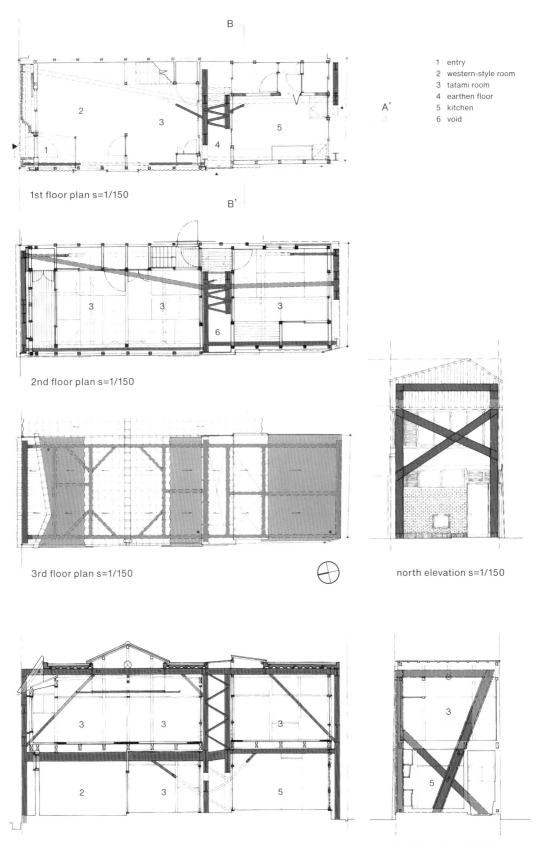

1 entry
2 western-style room
3 tatami room
4 earthen floor
5 kitchen
6 void

1st floor plan s=1/150

2nd floor plan s=1/150

3rd floor plan s=1/150

north elevation s=1/150

A-A' section s=1/150

B-B' section s=1/150

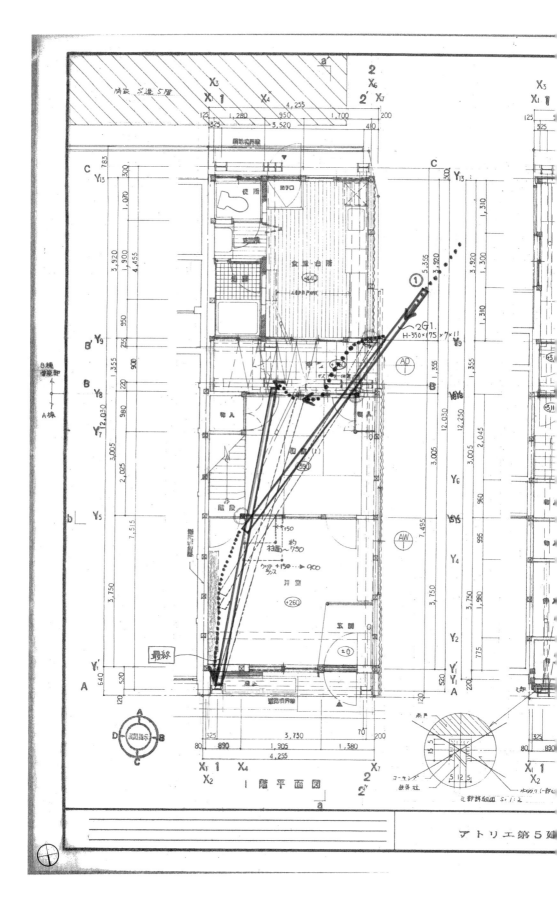

１階平面図

アトリエ第５建

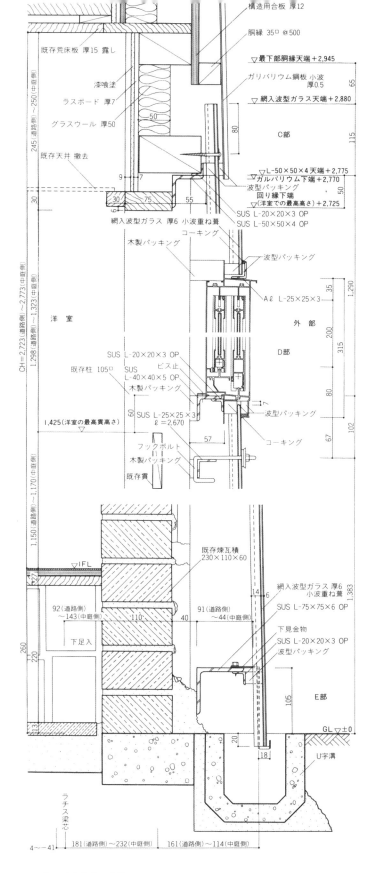

sectional detail s=1/6

土地の記憶を可視化する、
コンクリートの塊。
── 生活の背景。

A mass of concrete, visualizing the memory of the site.
── Background of life.

南芦屋浜団地コミュニティ&
アート計画 "Sacrificatio"

Sacrificatio: Community & Art Project for
Minami-Ashiyahama Public Housing Complex

1998

芦屋沖の埋立地に建設された、阪神淡路大震災の被災者向けの公営住宅団地の中に、古い防潮堤（p.80上）に姿を借りた海岸線の遺跡のような構造物をつくった。6つの住棟とその間の中庭を貫いて400mにわたって断続するコンクリートの塊は、新しい居住者にとって生活の背景となることを願ったものである。歴史的文脈を持たない平板な埋立地に、土地のさまざまな時間を、震災や水害といった負の記憶も含めてあらかじめ内包しようという意図である。海水面から正しい高さにある新しい「防潮堤」は、消えた海岸線と海面を可視化して、そこがかつて海であったことを想起させる。雁行する「防潮堤」の配置は、幾重にも重なる山ひだを映し取って、背後に聳える六甲山の気配を増幅する。皮肉にもそれは震災を引き起こした活断層と平行することを意味する。都市の記憶は常に重層的である。芦屋の埋立地もまたポジティブな意味において海岸線や海面の「犠牲」の上に獲得されている。

Located on the grounds of a public housing complex on reclaimed land off the coast of Ashiya, near Kobe, built for survivors of the Great Hanshin-Awaji Earthquake, this monument resembles the ruins of a vanished coastline and draws inspiration from an old coastal levee (p.80top). It was my hope that the ridges of concrete, which run intermittently for 400 meters through six tower blocks and the courtyards between them, would provide a living background for the new inhabitants. Here, on newly reclaimed land, flat and lacking historical context, this monument was intended to carry implications about the history and memory of the land we live on, including the dark legacy of disasters like earthquakes and floods. The monument is at the correct height for an actual levee, evoking the vanished coastline and sea surface while hinting at the fact that the site was once the sea. The series of parallel diagonal formations is reminiscent of layers upon layers of folds seen on mountainous terrain, echoing and amplifying the presence of Mt. Rokko, which forms a scenic backdrop to the region. Ironically, both the monuments and mountains run parallel to the active fault lines that caused the earthquake. The history of a city has many layers. Like other cities, the reclaimed area of Ashiya is, in a positive sense, built on the sacrifice of coastline and sea.

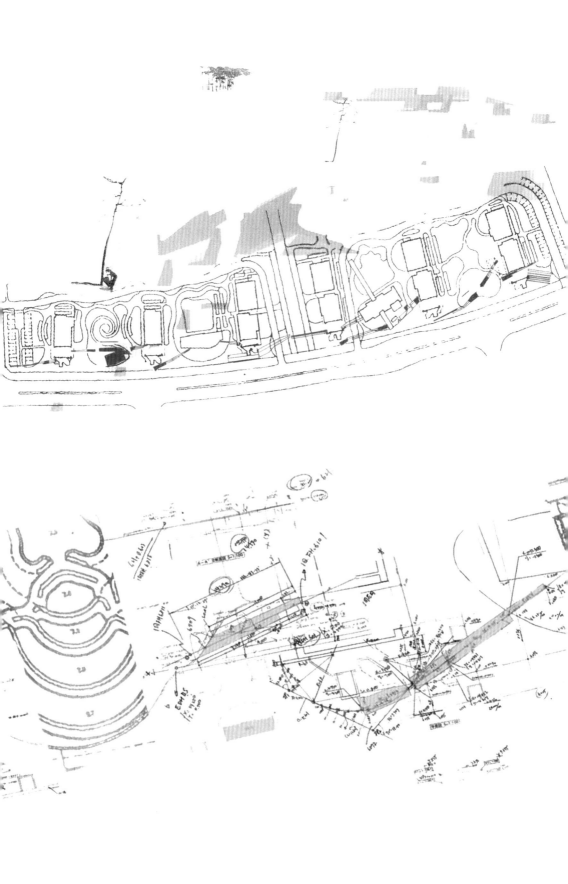

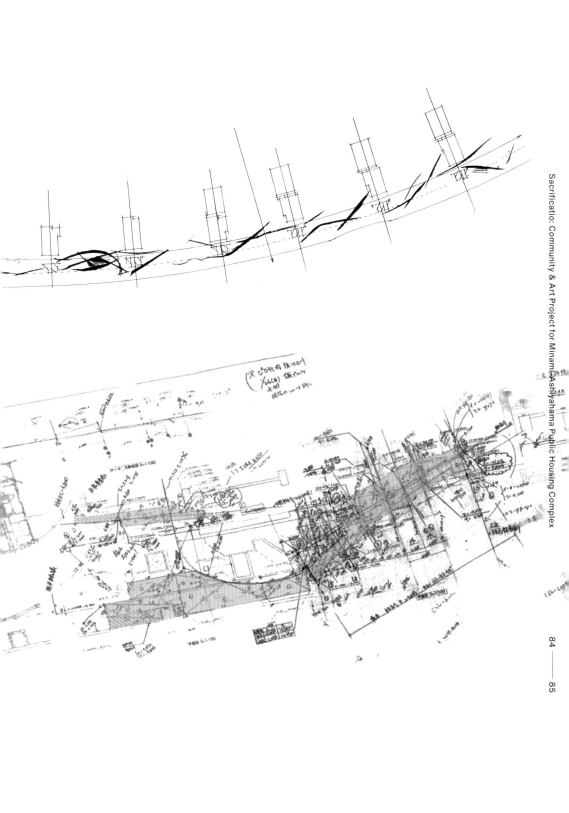

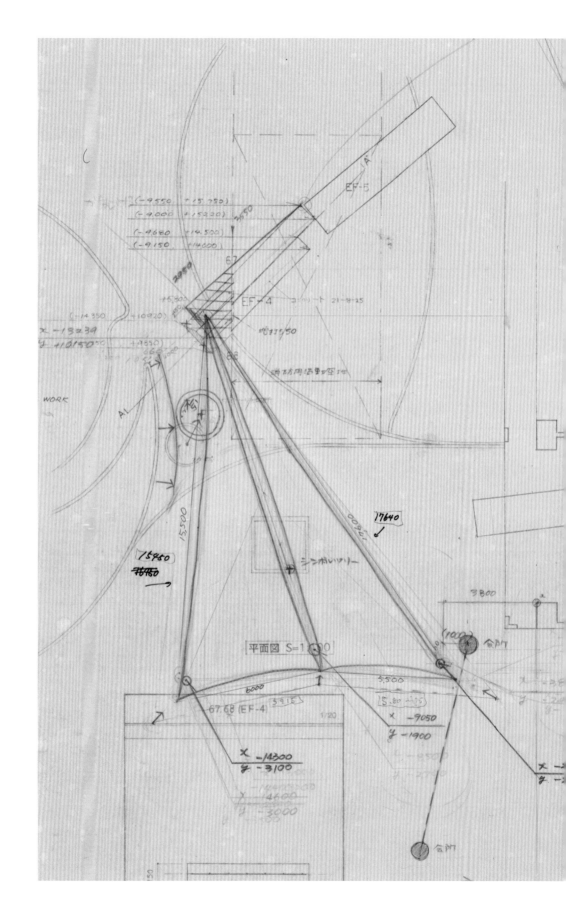

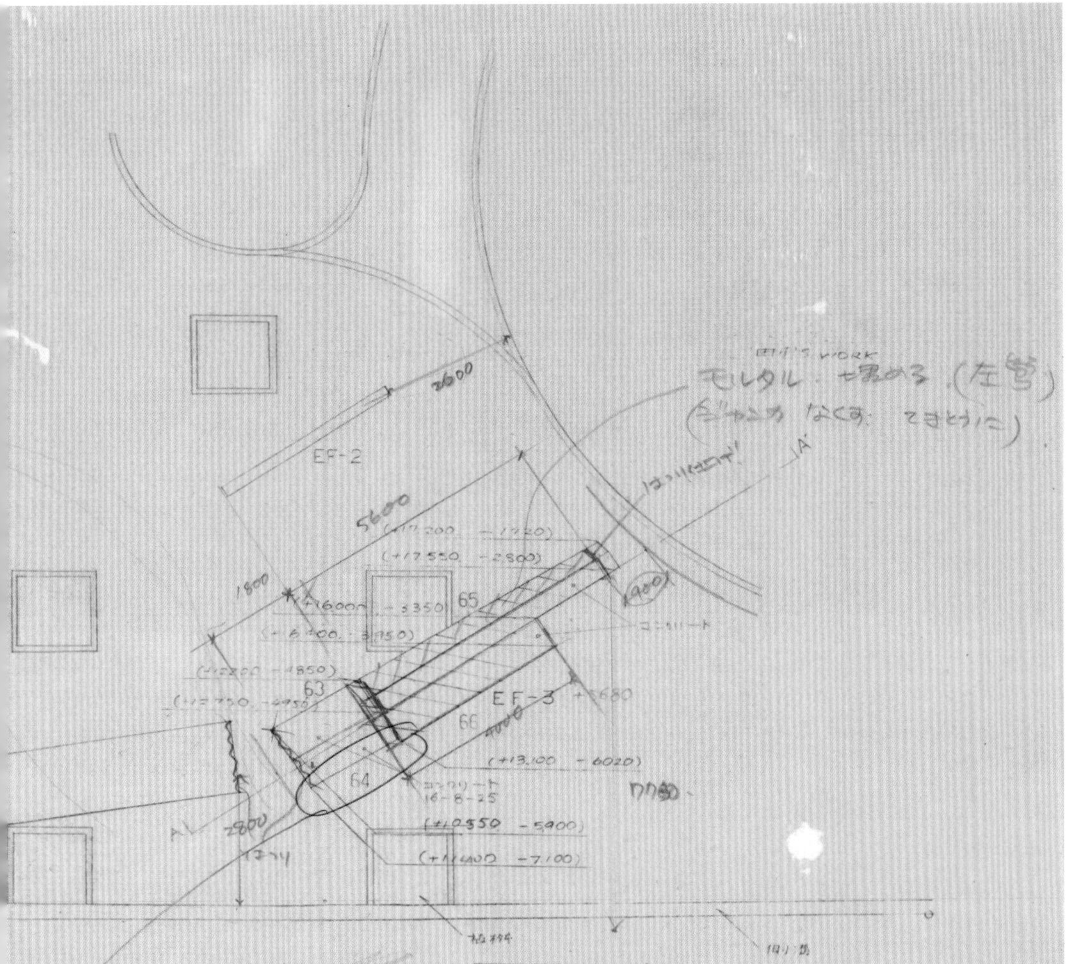

EF-2

モルタル・埋める（左官）
（ごちゃごちゃ なくす。てきとうに）

EF-3

平面図 S=1:100

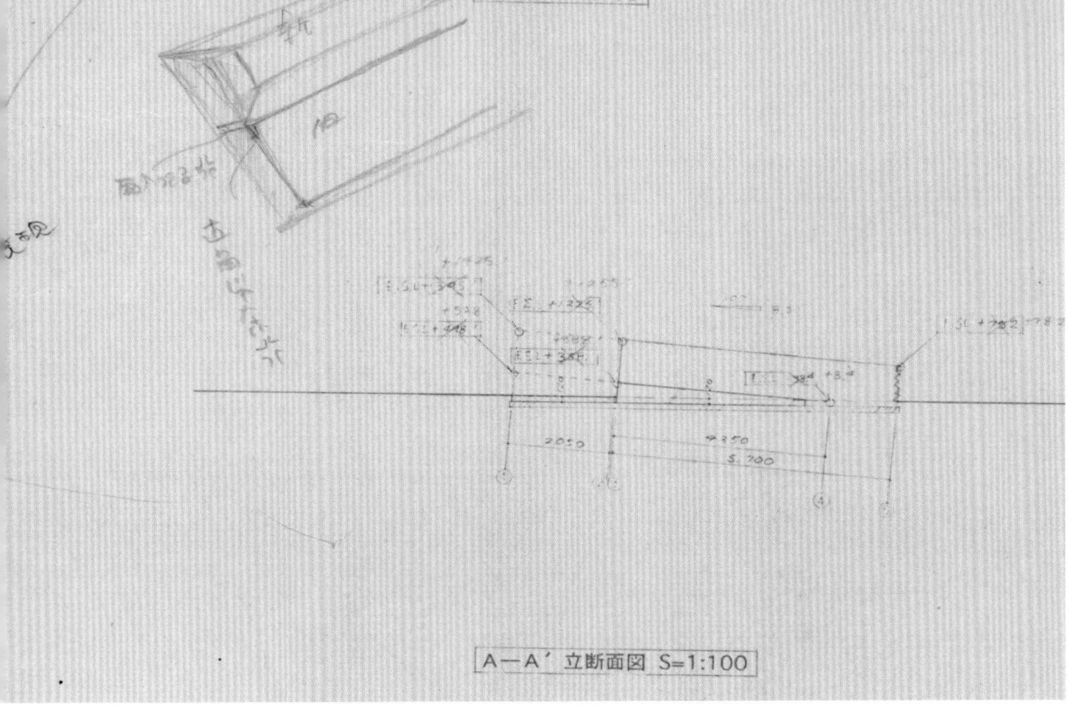

A—A' 立断面図 S=1:100

「環境のポケット」のような住宅。

A house like an "environmental pocket."

SH@64

1999

敷地は阪神淡路大震災後に指定された区画整理区域内にある。周辺の住宅は土地の減歩にともなって大半が3階建てとなり、パーキング以外にほぼオープンスペースを持たない。そんな風景の中に「環境のポケット」とでも呼べる住宅をつくりたいと考え、街並のスケール感を外すように、2階建てでありながら高さを実質1.5階建てくらいに低く抑えている。階高を詰めるために天井懐は設けず、2階床は剛床設計を兼ねて30mm厚の杉板一枚で構成した。薄い床に透過性材料を嵌め込みインナートップライトとすることにより、2階床は「自由な床」となり上下階の浸透を生み出すことになった。1階は、客間、食堂、台所、浴室といった合目的的かつパブリックな小部屋がルースに連続しており、全体として「土間」の様相を呈する。対照的に2階は固定壁のない「広間」として計画したが、L字平面が親子5人のための空間を可動間仕切りやカーテンによって分節するための有効な補助線として機能している。

The site is located in the "land readjustment areas" designated after the Great Hanshin-Awaji Earthquake. Most of the houses in the neighborhood are three-story buildings to compensate for the rezoning's reduction of land parcel sizes, and there are almost no open spaces other than parking lots. Within such context, I wanted to create a house that could be called an "environmental pocket," and in order to remove the sense of scale of the streetscape, I kept the height of the house to about 1.5 stories, even though it is a two-story building. No drop ceiling was installed to reduce the height of the second floor which is composed of single 30mm-thick cedar planks forming a "rigid floor design." By fitting translucent or transparent materials into the thin floor to create an inner top light, the second floor became a "free floor design" and created permeation between the upper and lower floors. The first floor is organized with a loose sequence of small public purpose-built small rooms such as the guest room, dining room, kitchen, and bathroom, and as a whole, it is reminiscent of an old-fashioned "earthen floor." In contrast, the second floor was planned as a "hall" without fixed walls, but the L-shaped plan allows for effective division of space for the five-person family using movable partitions and curtains.

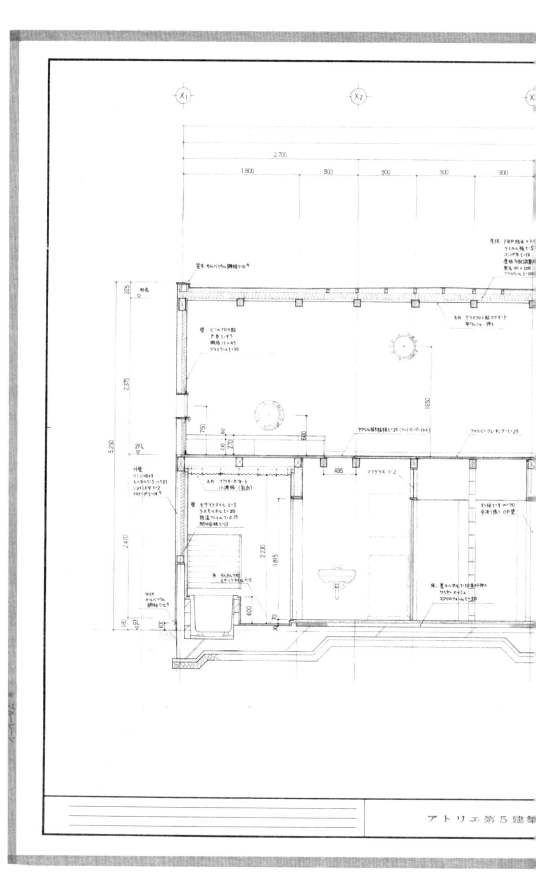

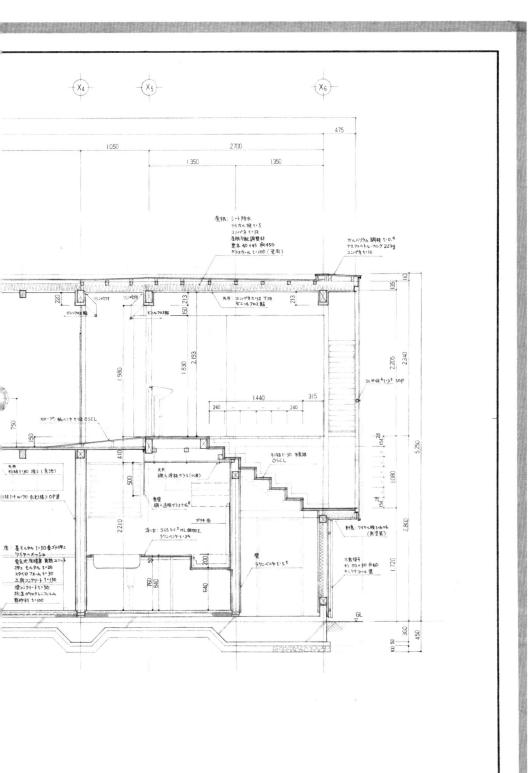

設計担当		縮 尺	工事名称	邸新築工事	A 13
		S=1:50			
		設計年月日	図面名称	矩 計 図 (2)	No.
		H11.6.11			

1 parking
2 entry
3 earthen floor
4 kitchen
5 dining room
6 guest room
7 storage
8 bathroom
9 court
10 hall (children)
11 hall (parents)
12 roof deck

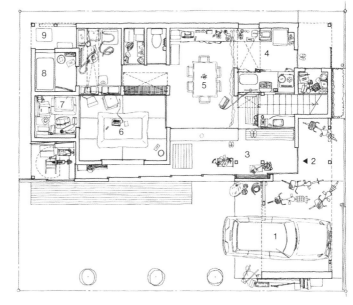

1st floor plan (after moving in) s=1/150

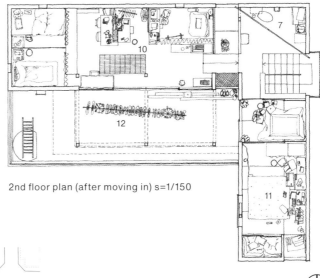

2nd floor plan (after moving in) s=1/150

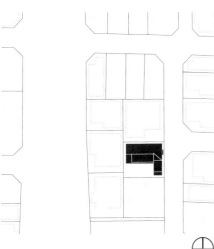

site plan   s=1:1200

線

S₁ S₂ S₃ S₄

900   2,000   1,000   1,000

5,000

屋根：
ガルバリウム鋼板 t=0.4 立てハ
アスファルトルーフィング22kg
構造用合板 t=12
母屋 40×45

屋根：
シート防水（非歩行用）
ケイカル板 t=5
コンパネ t=12
屋根勾配調整材
構造用合板 t=12
母屋 40×45

笠木：
コンクリート金ゴテ押エ

ロフト：
構造用合板 t=12 サンドペーパー仕上
根太 40×45

天井：
漆喰塗
石膏プラスター t=7.5
ラスボード t=7.5
構造用合板 t=12
グラスウール t=100

ロフト

G2A

構造用合板 t=12 サンドペーパー仕上

CH=504～976

天井：
構造用合板 t=12 サンドペーパー仕上
グラスウール t=100

壁：
ガルバリウム鋼板 スパンドレル
t=0.5 W=95
P.B t=12.5

頭繋：
シナベニヤ t=12 2K塗
根太 60×60

139.9   139.9

237.5

500

クリート打放シ
C1

天井：
漆喰塗
石膏プラスター t=9
ラスボード t=9.5
胴縁 15×45
グラスウール t=50

天井：
漆喰塗
石膏プラスター t=7.5
ラスボード t=7.5

階段（2）

廊下（3

普通型枠コンクリート打

便所（2）

CH=2,400

廊下（2）

CH=2,728～3,965

97

1,803 1,900 2,400

壁：
モザイクタイル貼

頭繋：
シナランバーコア t=36
頭繋：
シナランバーコア t=18

2FL

床：
桐縁甲板 t=15 エコワックス
根太 40×45 @360以内
大引 90×45

インナートップライト

床：
桐縁甲板 t=15 エコワックス
根太 40×45
大引 90×45

2SL

床：
強化ガラス t=10
（飛散防止フィルム マット調貼）

2,880

G1

237.5

G2A

天井：小幅板型枠 コンクリート打放シ

50 50
100

フロートガラス t=5
飛散防止フィルム貼（マット調）

St.fL 40×300 SOP塗

階段（1）

St.fL 40×300 SOP塗

階段：
シナランバーコア t=12 エコワックス
段板 St.fL t=6 斜面加工（溜込・上げ裏；SOP塗）
力桁 2C-150×50×20×3.2 SOP塗

洗面室

CH=2,650

CB t=100 磁丸積

倉庫

CH=2,650

C1a

壁：
モザイクタイル貼

カウンタートップ：
タモ集成材 t=30 UC

棚：
シナベニヤフラッシュ t=21
エコワックス

床：
桐縁甲板 t=15 エコワックス
根太 40×45 @360以内
グラスウール t=50
大引 90×45

頭繋：
シナラ

床：
ノーマンラバー Lタイプ t=3.3（ニチマン）貼
コンパネ t=12
根太 40×45 @360以内
グラスウール t=50
大引 90×45

下足箱

-150 (DPA-15)

砂利敷

FG2A

大引受金 プラボ ト (FL/UVI) @360以内

FG1a

2,000

捨コンクリート t=50
防湿ポリエチレンフィルム t=0.15
耐圧石 t=100

X₁   X₂   X₃

敷地が持つ可能性を構造体で再定義する。

Redefine a site's potential with structures.

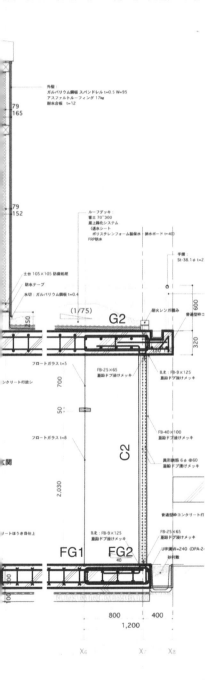

外壁：
ガルバリウム鋼板 スパンドレル t=0.5 W=95
アスファルトルーフィング 17kg
耐水合板 t=12

79
165

79
152

ルーフデッキ：
客土 70~300
屋上緑化システム
（透水シート
ポリスチレンフォーム製保水・排水ボード t=40）
FRP防水

土台 105×105 防蟻処理
防水テープ
水切：ガルバリウム鋼板 t=0.4

手摺：
St-38.1φ t=2

(1/75)

G2

耐火レンガ積み

普通型鋼 叮一

600

50

320

普通コンクリート 打放シ

フロートガラス t=5

FB-25×65
亜鉛ドブ漬けメッキ

B.R：FB-9×125
亜鉛ドブ漬けメッキ

700

150 150

ンクリート打放シ

50

FB-40×100
亜鉛ドブ漬けメッキ

フロートガラス t=8

C2

2,030

真形鉄筋 6φ @60
亜鉛ドブ漬けメッキ

玄関

普通型鋼W=240 叮コンクリート 打

ートほうき目仕上

FG1   FG2

B.R：FB-9×125
亜鉛ドブ漬けメッキ

FB-25×65
亜鉛ドブ漬けメッキ

UFP溝鋼W=240 (DPA-2-40)
砂利敷

800   400

1,200

X6   X7   X8

ヒ

2000

「ヒ」という名称は2枚のスラブと1枚の壁で構成されたヒの字型断面のRC躯体に因む。設計に当たっては、ストラクチュアによって敷地を「宅地」という最大限利用可能なインフラストラクチュアにつくり直すことから始めた。「宅地」化のための設計条件として以下が求められた。①特別な事情から、西側隣地との関係を建築的に遮断する。②1階を中心とした生活を、庭もろとも日当たりのよい2階に持ち上げる。③前面道路から庭への視線の抜けを確保する。これらの条件に応えるインフラとして構想したのがヒの字型断面の人工地盤であり、そこに木造平屋を上下2段に独立して載せることで住宅を構成している。木造部分はRC躯体への差し掛け構造であり耐震壁を必要としない。2階のメインの棟の軸を振ることにより、隣接するお兄さん宅の日照や眺望を妨げない、庭を中心とした囲み配置や、アトリエの採光面として高さが必要な北側ファサードの圧迫感の低減などを実現している。

The building name ' ヒ ' refers to the reinforced concrete structure shaped like the *katakana* character ' ヒ ', which is composed of two floor slabs and one wall slab. The design process began with the redevelopment of the site into "residential land," an infrastructural structure that could be used to its fullest extent. In creating "residential land," three points linked to various environmental conditions were prioritized: 1-To construct a barrier on the west side, a response to on-going issues with the neighbor; 2-To move the typically first-floor functions up to the sunny second-floor, including the garden; 3-To secure a clear line of sight from the front road to the garden. The infrastructure meeting these conditions was conceived as a ' ヒ '-shaped cross-section forming artificial ground floors, and on each floor, an independent single-story wooden house was constructed. The wooden structure is attached to the RC wall and does not require earthquake-resistant walls. By shifting the axis of the main wing on the second floor, the house is arranged around the garden so as not to obstruct the sunlight and view for the adjacent brother's house, while also reducing the oppressive feeling of the tall north façade required to provide light for the atelier.

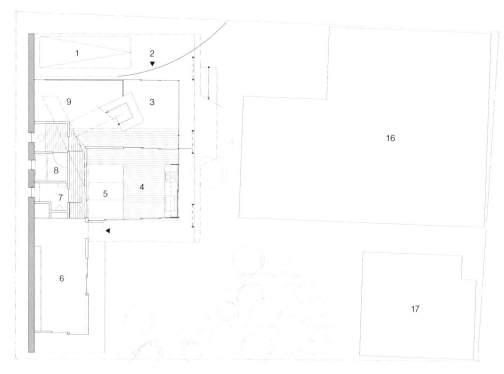

1st floor plan s=1/200

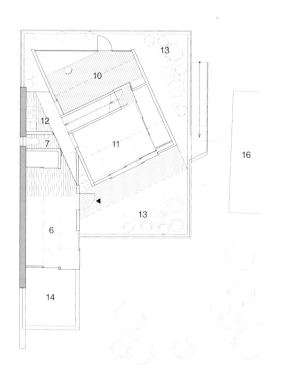

1 parking
2 porch
3 entrance hall
4 dining-kitchen
5 tatami space
6 bedroom
7 WC
8 bathroom
9 storage
10 atelier
11 tatami room
12 kichenette
13 roof deck
14 terrace
15 loft
16 brother's house
17 gallery

2nd floor plan s=1/200

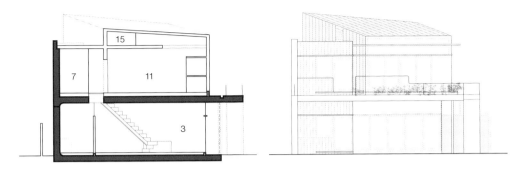

east-west section s=1/200

south elevation s=1/200

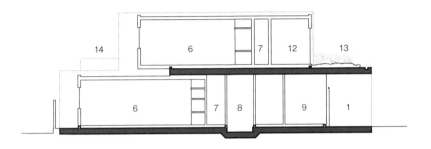

south-north section s=1/200

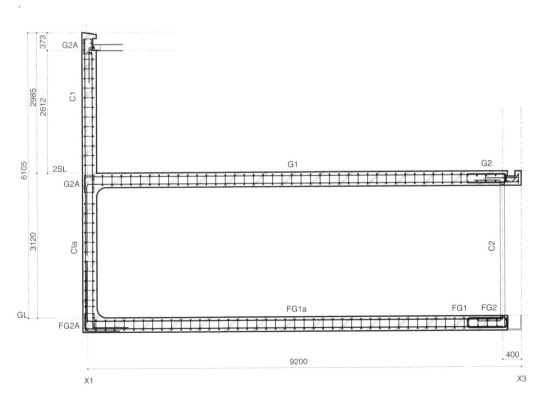

rebar arrangement drawing s=1/80

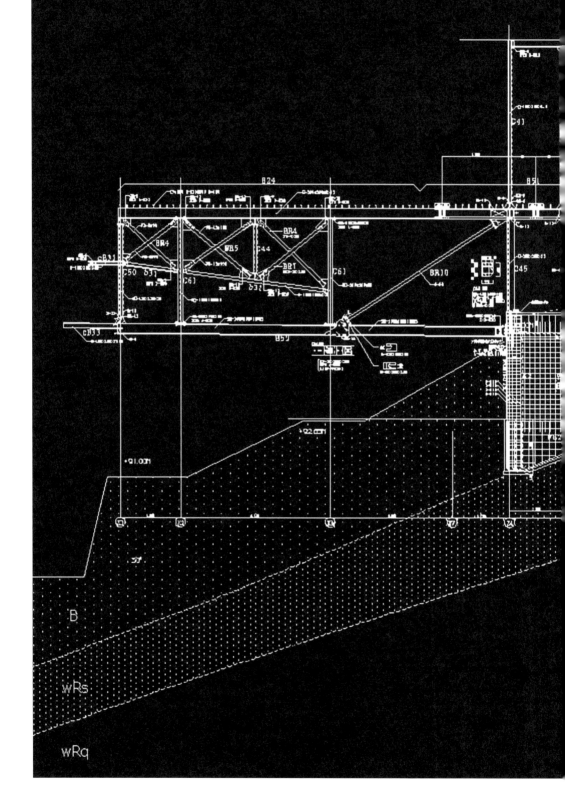

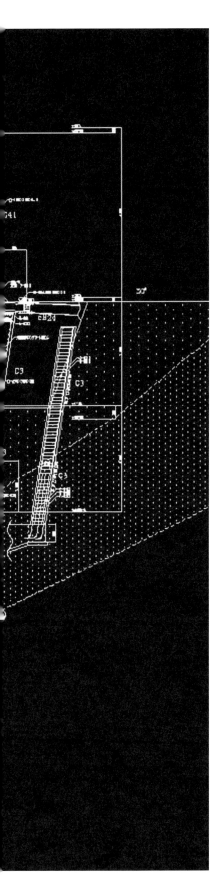

斜面地特有の景観を
余す所なく使い倒す。

Fully utilize the unique sloping terrain landscapes.

苦楽園
KURAKUEN

2001

平均斜度が30°を超える急斜面に建つ住宅である。貴重な平場は庭として利用し、むしろ斜面部分を選んで建築を配置し、支持地盤に達する強固な基礎を設けて荷重を集中させている。ランダムに傾いた斜柱群に支えられた1階ヴォリュームは、道路レベルと庭を結ぶスロープが構造的に「たが」のように働いて安定的に空中に張り出している。インテリアは斜面地特有の景観を取り込んで構成している。例えば、書斎からは人口1000万人を擁するエリアのパノラマを楽しめる。岩山が露出したピロティと連続する居間は、グレーの人造石研出しで仕上げた穴蔵風の空間である。キャンティレバーの先端に置いたモザイクタイル貼りの造形風呂では、斜面下の雑木林の樹冠に抱かれているかのような錯覚を覚える。地階に隠された寝室は樹木にバウンドした柔らかな緑色の光に包まれる空間であり、そのインテリアは全面ガラス越しに、巨石積みの石垣、斜柱群と背後の雑木林によって構成されている。

This house is built on a steep terrain with an average slope of over 30 degrees. The valuable flat area is used as a garden, and the building is placed on the slope instead, with a rigid foundation that reaches the supporting rock bed to concentrate the load. The first-floor volume, supported by a group of randomly inclined leaning pillars, is structurally "hooped" by the ramp connecting the garden to the street level, resulting in a stable cantilever in the air. The interior is designed to incorporate the unique landscape of the sloping terrain. For example, the study offers a panoramic view of an area with a population of 10 million. The living room, which is connected to the uncovered rocky terrain 'pilotis', is a cave-like space finished with gray terrazzo. The mosaic-tiled bathroom at the end of the cantilever creates the illusion of being embraced by the forest canopy from below. The bedroom, hidden under the first floor, is a space enveloped in soft green light reflected off the trees; its interior is fully enclosed in glass, nestled among stacked megalithic natural stone walls and a group of leaning pillars accompanied by the grove of trees behind them.

Esquisse-Atelier

991228-a | Architect Client

000105 | Esquisse-

Esquisse-Atelier

991228-b | Architect Client

000107 | Esquisse-

Architect Client

991228-b | Architect Client

000108 | Architect Cl

Architect Client

991228-b | Architect Client

000108 | Esquisse-

Architect Client

991229 | Esquisse-Atelier

000108 | Esquisse-

Esquisse Atelier

000105

Esquisse Atelier

000108

10   Esquisse-Atelier

000119   Esquisse-Atelier

000124   E

15   Esquisse-Atelier

000119   Esquisse-Atelier

000125   E

KURAKUEN

16   Architect Client

000120   Esquisse-Atelier

000125   E

117   Esquisse-Atelier

000120   Architect Client

000125   Arch

18   Esquisse-Atelier

000124   Esquisse-Atelier

000125   Arch

118   Architect Client

000124   Esquisse-Atelier

000129

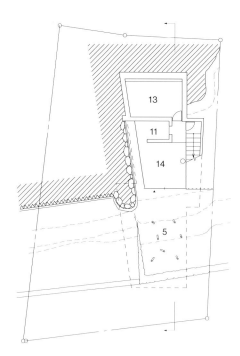

basement floor plan s=1/300

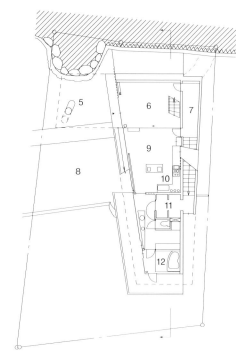

1st floor plan s=1/300

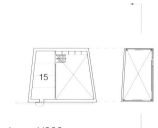

loft plan s=1/300

site plan s=1:1000

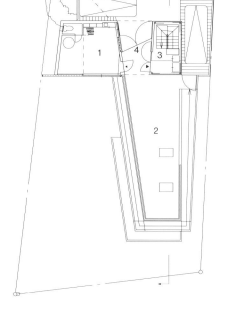

2nd floor plan s=1/300

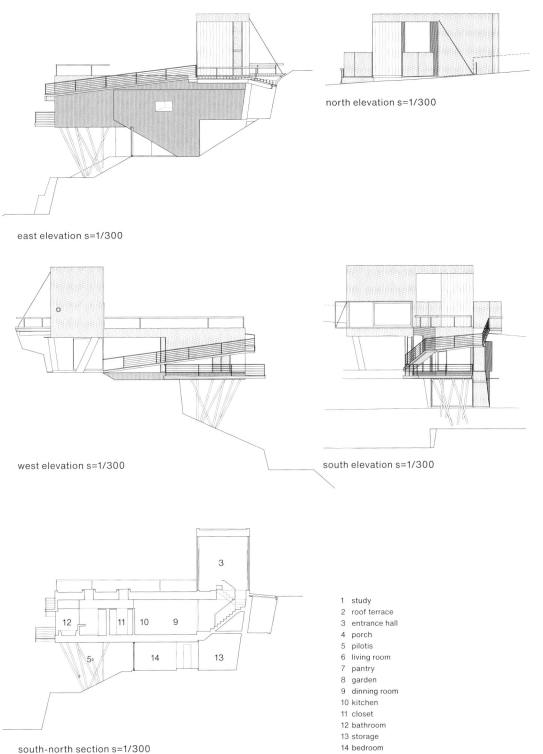

north elevation s=1/300

east elevation s=1/300

west elevation s=1/300

south elevation s=1/300

south-north section s=1/300

1   study
2   roof terrace
3   entrance hall
4   porch
5   pilotis
6   living room
7   pantry
8   garden
9   dinning room
10 kitchen
11 closet
12 bathroom
13 storage
14 bedroom
15 loft

苦楽園の増築
KURAKUEN Addition
2003

普段は広い犬小屋であり、時にはパーティールームとしても使用可能なアウトドア・リビングの計画である。施主の与件は、冬にはエアタイトが可能で、夏には風が通る一方で虫の侵入を防ぎ、中間期には全てが視界から消える、そんな魔法のような建具でピロティを囲うことであった。しかし現実の敷地は、岩の張り出し、大形サッシュの戸袋、異なる投影面を持つ天井と床、さらには隣地境界線の近接など大変複雑である。これら全ての条件に応えるために、コノイド曲面を描く半透明テント膜とネット膜を重ねた膜構造を採用した。2枚の膜はファスナーによって重ね着のように脱着が可能であり、開口部も軽く開け閉めすることができる。洋服のような軽い増築である。

The plan is for an outdoor living room that will normally shelter the family dog but can also serve as a party room at times. The client's brief was to enclose the 'pilotis' with magic-like fixtures that would be airtight in the winter, breezy but insect-free in the summer, and could be stowed out of sight in the interim. But the actual site is very complicated; there were jutting rocks, a shutter case for a large sliding door, ceilings and floors with different projection surfaces, its proximity to the boundary of the adjacent property, and much more. In order to fulfill these conditions, a conoid curved membrane structure consisting of a translucent tent and net was employed. The two membranes are removable layer by layer with zippers, and the openings can be opened and closed lightly as well. It is a "light extension," like a piece of clothing.

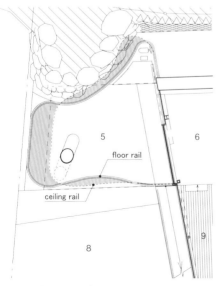

5

6

floor rail

ceiling rail

8

9

1st floor plan s=1/150

苦楽園の離れ
KURAKUEN Annex
2008

『苦楽園の増築』のさらに5年後に『苦楽園の離れ』を増築した。敷地はすでに尽きたかに思われたが、施主が庭から一段下った急斜面の中にわずかな平地を発見し、木造で小さな小屋をつくった。主な用途は新たな書斎である。ルーフデッキは、寝室前のデッキへと至る階段の大きな踊り場でもあり、庭の延長として利用される。ルーフデッキに置かれたテーブルは、書斎のトップライトを立ち上げたものである。

Five years after 'KURAKUEN Addition', I added this annex. I had thought there was no more buildable land on the site, but the owner found a small flat area surrounded by a steep slope, at a level lower than the garden, and a small wooden shed was built. The main use of the shed is a new study. Its roof deck is also the large landing for the stairs leading to the deck in front of the bedroom and is used as an extension of the garden. The table on the roof deck is a raised top light for the study.

屋根の載せ替えだけによる、面積の増えない「大増築」。

A "large extension" with no increase in area by simply replacing the roof.

スガルカラハフ
SUGARUKARAHAFU

2002

庫裏とは寺院に付属する僧侶の住まいであるが、このプロジェクトはさらにその庫裏に副住職家族のための小住宅を増築するものである。増築には、ただ床面積が増えるという以上のメリットがほしい。ここでは増床は必要最小限にとどめて、既存の緩い寄棟屋根を大きく照りのついた片流れ屋根に載せ替えることで、その下で展開される生活を根本的に再構成しようと考えた。屋根を載せ替える当初の目的は、リビングに十分な日照を得ることであった。しかし高くなった天井高を利用してロフトを計画したところ、庫裏の大きな銅板葺き屋根が突然、ロフトの延長として感じられるようになった。それが「屋根の部屋」と呼ぶ内外一体となった空間である。日本の社寺建築には、縋破風という屋根の増築についての優れたデザイン手法がある。ここでは新設屋根に「縋る」かたちで藤棚を設けている。藤棚とは、つまりは空の破風である。合わせて「スガルカラハフ」である。

The word *Kuri* refers to a residence for a Buddhist priest, annexed to a temple. Here, a small house for the family of the vice priest was added to an existing *Kuri*. But one should expect more advantages than just the enlargement of floor area with an extension. The idea here was to keep the additional floor to a minimum and replace the existing gently inclined hipped roof with a shed roof that is curved toward the sky, thus radically reconfiguring the life that unfolds beneath it. The primary purpose of replacing the roof was to provide sufficient daylight for the living room. However, when a loft was planned to take advantage of the increased ceiling height, the large copper-shingled roof of the *Kuri* suddenly began to feel like an extension of the floor of the loft. The space where the interior and exterior are brought together as a whole is called the "roof room." In the architecture of Japanese shrines and temples, there is an excellent design technique for roof extensions called *sugaruhafu* which means clinging gable. Here, we placed a wisteria trellis to "cling" to the newly constructed shed roof. The wisteria trellis, in other words, is an empty (*kara*) gable (*hafu*). The combination of these keywords gave the house its name, 'SUGARUKARAHAFU'.

1 'SUGARUKARAHAFU'
2 dining room
3 living room
4 bedroom
5 study
6 roof terrace
7 room with roof
8 slanting terrace
(existing roof)

extension

renovation

1st floor plan s=1/250

loft floor plan s=1/250

section s=1/250

west elevation s=1/250

before

建築だけでなく、
生活と研究を支える一枚の壁。

A single wall that supports not only architecture,
but also life and research.

SoHo

2003

郊外型のSOHOである。クライアントである言語学者夫妻のために、ラボと呼ぶ研究スペースを最下階の土間に設けている。ラボはエントランスホールと応接間としての機能を合わせ持ち、さらにDKもラボの領域に含まれる。断面構成としては、上下二段に分かれていた敷地の高低差を上方に延長するようにスキップフロアーを5層重ねている。空気的には大きな一室空間であるが、階を上がるにしたがってプライバシーの度合が高まり、次第に寛いだ雰囲気になるように計画している。一室空間全体を見渡すアングルは存在せず、視線はラボ⇆DK⇆リビング⇆寝室⇆ロフトと反射をくり返しながら上下する。4つある階段は上部のものほど傾斜が緩い。北側の壁全面がさまざまな用途に対応した収納壁となっており、生活の背景となる一枚の連続するインテリアとして上下階をつないでいる。収納壁の鉄板製の仕切り板は主要な構造体としても機能しており、南面を大きく開放することに寄与している。

This is a suburban-type live-work setting called SOHO (Small Office/Home Office) in Japan. For the client, a couple who are both linguists, I planned a research space called the "lab," located on a dirt floor at the bottom. The lab functions as an entrance hall and reception room as well, while the dining and kitchen (DK) are also included in the lab area. In terms of the cross-sectional composition, 5 layers of skipped floors were set based on the existing level difference of the double-tiered site. Although planned within a shared air volume and as a large single-room space, the degree of privacy increases as one moves up the floors, creating a gradually more relaxed atmosphere. There are no viewpoints that overlook the entire space, and the eye moves up and down, back and forth from the lab ⇆ DK ⇆ living room ⇆ bedroom ⇆ loft, respectively. The slope is gentler at the top of the four staircases. The entire north wall is turned into a multi-purpose storage wall, connecting the upper and lower floors, forming a continuous interior, and acting as a background of life. The steel plate partitions of the storage wall also function as the main structural elements, contributing to the large open southern façade.

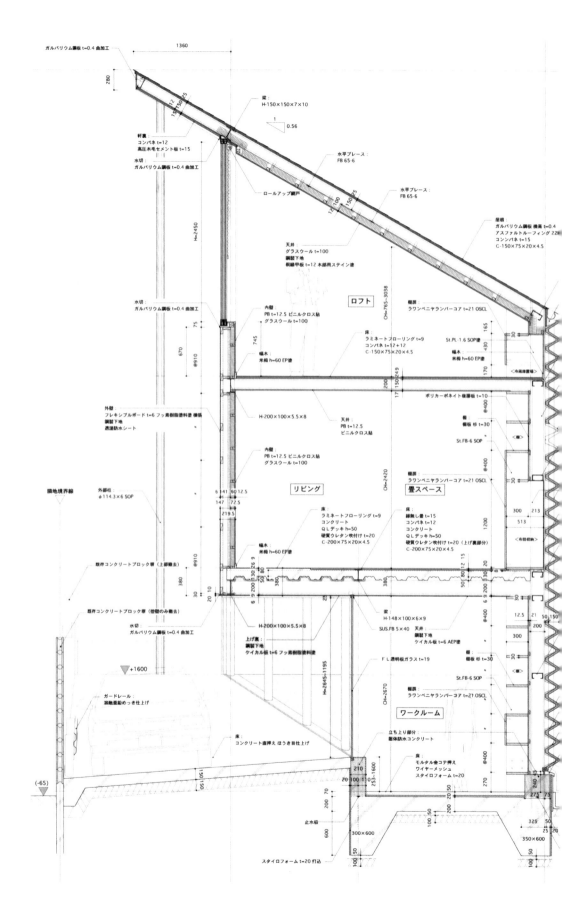

ガルバリウム鋼板 t=0.4 曲加工

1360

280

ガルバリウム鋼板 t=0.4 曲加工

1 150 25
12

梁：
H-150×150×7×10

1
0.56

軒裏：
コンパネ t=12
高圧木毛セメント板 t=15

水切：
ガルバリウム鋼板 t=0.4 曲加工

水平ブレース：
FB 65-6

ロールアップ網戸

水平ブレース：
FB 65-6

12 100 150 25

屋根：
ガルバリウム鋼板 横葺 t=0.4
アスファルトルーフィング 22K
コンパネ t=15
C-150×75×20×4.5

H=2450

天井：
グラスウール t=100
鋼製下地
桐縁甲板 t=12 木部用ステイン塗

ロフト

CH=765-3038

棚扉：
ラワンベニヤランバーコア t=21 OSCL

水切：
ガルバリウム鋼板 t=0.4 曲加工

75

内壁：
PB t=12.5 ビニルクロス貼
・グラスウール t=100

床：
ラミネートフローリング t=9
コンパネ t=12＋12
C-150×75×20×4.5

St.PL.1.6 SOP塗

米栂 h=60 EP塗

@910

670

幅木
米栂 h=60 EP塗

〈冷蔵庫置場〉

745

200 17 150 249

ポリカーボネイト積層板 t=10

棚：
棚板 杉 t=30

外壁：
フレキシブルボード t=6 フッ素樹脂塗料塗 横張
鋼製下地
透湿防水シート

H-200×100×5.5×8

天井：
PB t=12.5
ビニルクロス貼

CH=2420

St.FB-6 SOP

〈棚〉

@400

内壁：
PB t=12.5 ビニルクロス貼
グラスウール t=100

隣地境界線

外部柱：
φ114.3×6 SOP

6 141 60 12.5
147 72.5
219.5

リビング

畳スペース

棚扉：
ラワンベニヤランバーコア t=21 OSCL

1200

300 213

幅木
米栂 h=60 EP塗

床：
ラミネートフローリング t=9
コンクリート
QLデッキ h=50
硬質ウレタン吹付け t=20
C-200×75×20×4.5

床：
縁無し畳 t=15
コンパネ t=12
コンクリート
QLデッキ h=50
硬質ウレタン吹付け t=20 (上げ裏部分)
C-200×75×20×4.5

513

〈布団収納〉

@910

380

@400

30

既存コンクリートブロック塀 (上部撤去)

30 20 10

H-200×100×5.5×8

6 9 200 130 26 9
50 80

380

梁：
H-148×100×6×9

SUS.FB 5×40

380

6 9 200 50 80 12 15
30

12.5 21 50 150
200

既存コンクリートブロック塀 (捨壁のみ撤去)

水切：
ガルバリウム鋼板 t=0.4 曲加工

▽+1600

上げ裏：
鋼製下地
ケイカル板 t=6 フッ素樹脂塗料塗

天井：
鋼製下地
ケイカル板 t=6 AEP塗

300

棚：
棚板 杉 t=30

ガードレール：
溶融亜鉛めっき仕上げ

H=2645-1195

CH=2670

FL透明板ガラス t=19

St.FB-6 SOP

30

棚扉：
ラワンベニヤランバーコア t=21 OSCL

ワークルーム

@400

床：
コンクリート直押え ほうき目仕上げ

立上り部分：
躯体防水コンクリート

床：
モルタル金コテ押え
ワイヤーメッシュ
スタイロフォーム t=20

240 30

272 75

(-65)

210
52 100 110
253-1600

200 20 50

100 50
200

200 70

止水板

600

300×600

325
350×600

スタイロフォーム t=20 打込

100

50

100 50

50

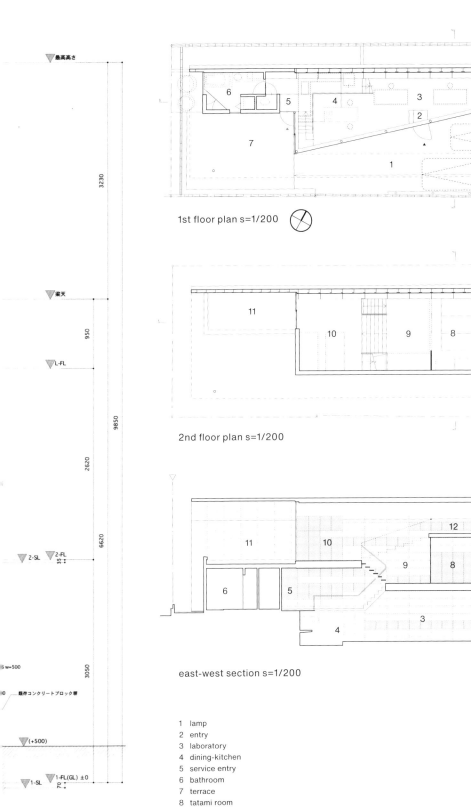

1st floor plan s=1/200

2nd floor plan s=1/200

east-west section s=1/200

1 lamp
2 entry
3 laboratory
4 dining-kitchen
5 service entry
6 bathroom
7 terrace
8 tatami room
9 living room
10 bedroom
11 roof terrace
12 loft

「封印」された地下空間を
「覚醒」させる。

"Awakening" a "sealed" underground space.

湊町アンダーグラウンドプロジェクト
Minatomachi Underground Project

2003

大阪市の中心部JR難波駅近くに眠る、「なにわトンネル」と名付けられた手つかずの巨大地下空間を利用したアートプロジェクトである。「なにわトンネル」はパースペクティブがついた全長190mの細長い空間で、幅は25mから9mまで連続的に変化する。周辺の開発が進めば駅コンコースの延長として地下通路などに利用される計画であるが、実際には直下を走る鉄道トンネルのために立体的に生じたヘタ地として10年近く使われず、文字通り封印された状態であった。偶然この空間の存在を知り、アーティストと協働して光と映像によって場所を覚醒させる展示とその会場構成を行なった。高橋匡太は1232本の蛍光灯をパースペクティブの焦点に置いて圧倒的な光をつくり、映像ユニット"seesaw"と宮本のチームは床・壁・天井・柱・梁といったエレメントに対して区別なく、均質で無意味な映像を壁紙のように用いたプロジェクションを行った。異形の空間自体を意識化する試みである。

This was an art event held in a cavernous, unused underground space called Naniwa Tunnel, which slumbers beneath the city near JR Namba Station in central Osaka. Naniwa Tunnel is a long, narrow enclosure, 190 meters in length and varying in width from 9 to 25 meters, which rather resembles an illustration of one-point perspective. The space, formed carelessly as a result of work on an underground railway tunnel directly beneath it, was scheduled to be repurposed as a subterranean pedestrian walkway when the surrounding environment was developed, but it was actually sealed off and left unused for nearly 10 years. By chance I came to know of its existence and collaborated with artists on a plan to "awaken" the sleeping space with light-based installations. Kyota Takahashi generated dazzling light at the perspectival focal point using 1,232 fluorescent tubes, while the video art unit "seesaw" and the Miyamoto team projected imagery on the floor, walls, ceiling, columns, and beams, evenly like wallpaper, devoid of meaning. The project showcased this fascinatingly deformed urban space, bringing it into the light of awareness, perhaps for the first time.

33

敷地に呼応して、
建築を湾曲、かつ浮揚させる。

In response to the site,
the architecture is curved and floated.

SHIP

2006

3mの高低差を持つ、上下二段に造成された敷地に建つ住宅である。下段のうち信頼性の高い地盤部分を選んで基礎を設置し、そこから擁壁を飛び越えて眺めのよい上段の上空にリビングのヴォリュームを浮かべている。一方、個室については落ち着いた雰囲気の下段に配置し、張り出したヴォリュームと構造上のバランスをとっている。湾曲した壁の平面形は「く」の字に折れた敷地形状に呼応したものであり、12mm厚のコールテン鋼板を溶接してつくっている。船と同様のシームレスな構造体によって鉄板シェル構造を構成し、8mのキャンティレバーを効果的に支持している。上段レベルにはエントランスホールと予備室1室を設けただけで、ピロティ〜ポーチ〜ルーフデッキと半屋外空間が連続するヴォイドの多い構成となっている。結果的に、車室を挟んで上下に客室と浮体が離れて配置されるフェリーボートの船体に大変よく似た構成と構造を持つことになった。SHIPという名前の由来である。

The house is built on a site developed on two levels with a 3-meter difference. The foundation is placed on the lower level, where the ground is more reliable, while the living volume floats over the retaining wall and above the upper level for a better view. The private rooms, on the other hand, are placed at the lower level, where they have a calm atmosphere, and are structurally balanced with the overhanging volume. The curved wall plan is a response to the folded-shaped site and is made of 12 mm-thick COR-TEN steel plates welded together. The steel plate shell structure is composed of a seamless structure similar to that of a ship, effectively supporting the 8-meter cantilever. The upper level only has an entrance hall and one spare room, composed of many voids with a continuous semi-outdoor space from the 'pilotis' to the porch to the roof deck. As a result, it has a configuration and structure very similar to the hull of a ferryboat, with the passenger cabin above and the floatation body below, separated by the car deck. This is the origin of the name 'SHIP'.

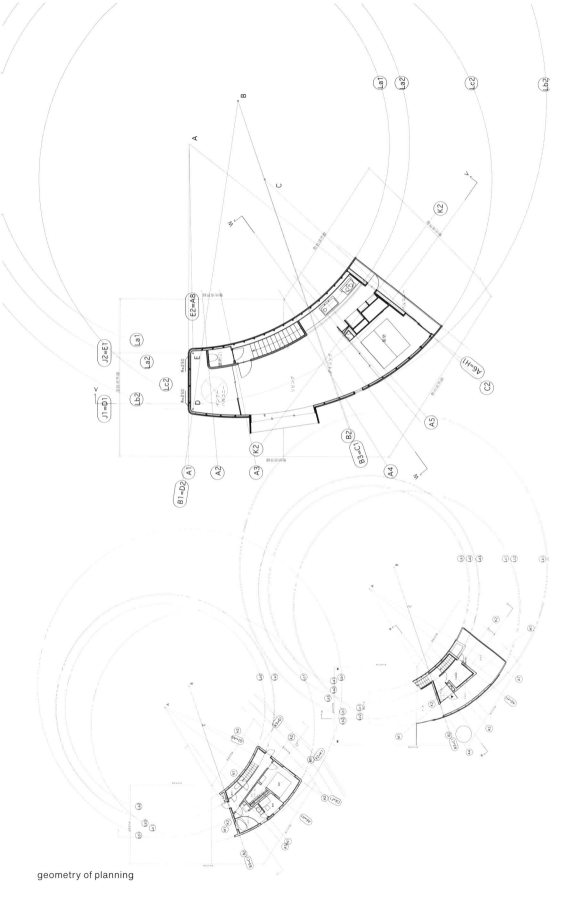

geometry of planning

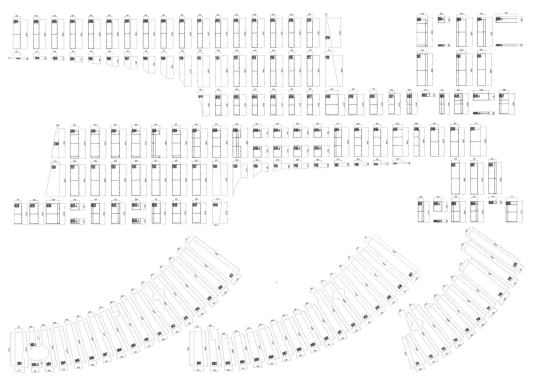

paneling of steel plate

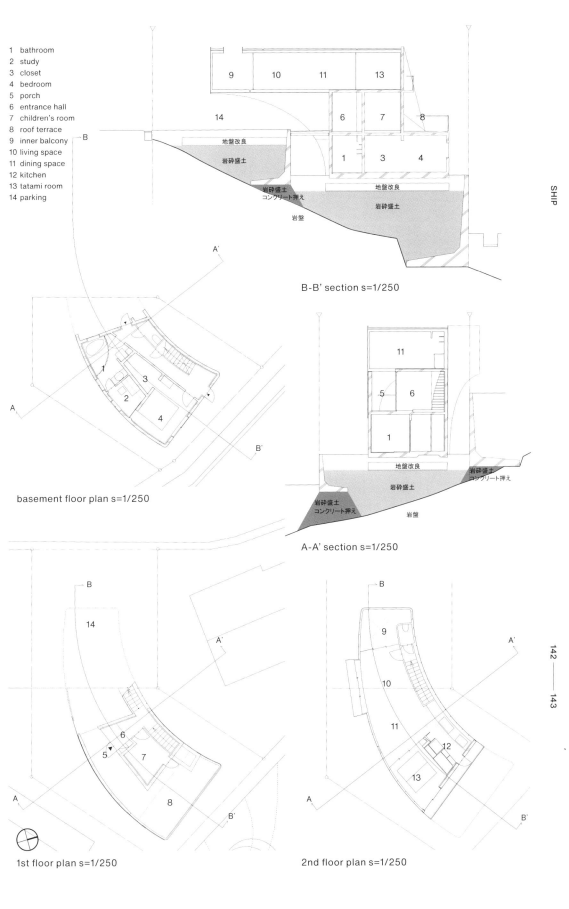

1 bathroom
2 study
3 closet
4 bedroom
5 porch
6 entrance hall
7 children's room
8 roof terrace
9 inner balcony
10 living space
11 dining space
12 kitchen
13 tatami room
14 parking

B-B' section s=1/250

basement floor plan s=1/250

A-A' section s=1/250

1st floor plan s=1/250

2nd floor plan s=1/250

「ヘタ地」を逆手にとり、
隣地の隅を拝借する。
——敷地の錬金術。

Converting an "irregular site" into an advantage,
borrowing corners of a neighboring lot.
——The alchemy within a site.

grappa
2006

狭小な直角三角形のヘタ地に建つ住宅である。壁面後退と北側斜線によって規定される最大ヴォリュームから、隅切りという単純な操作のみによって有効なオープンスペースと開口部を確保しようと試みた。隅切りによって敷地の端にできるオープンスペースは、それだけでは新たに小ぶりなヘタ地を生むに過ぎない。しかし目を敷地外に転じて、隣地の隅に残されたオープンスペース群と合わせて一体のものとして意識することができれば、突如ひとまとまりの有効なオープンスペースとして機能し始める。隣地の地型は矩形であるため、このオープンスペースに向かって隣家の主要な開口部が設けられることは通常あり得ない。即ちこの錬金術的借景は三角形ヘタ地にとっての必然であり力であるといえる。残り物には福がある。いやそれ以上かもしれない。ワインの搾りかすを集めて、蒸留し、発酵させて、手間をかけて美味しいものができ上がる。グラッパという名称の由来である。

This house is built on a narrow, right-angled triangular plot of *heta-chi* (left-over land). From the maximum volume defined by the wall setback and the north-facing diagonal line building limit, I attempted to secure effective open spaces and openings only through the simple operation of corner cutting. The open space created at the edge of the site due to the corner cuts could only result in small-sized, triangular plots of *heta-chi*. However, if we cast our gaze outside the site and become aware of it as an integral part of the open spaces left at the corners of neighboring lots, it suddenly begins to function as a unified and effective open space. Because of the rectangular shape of the adjoining lot, it is usually impossible to have the main openings of the neighboring house facing this spare open space. In other words, this alchemical *shakkei* (borrowed landscape) is the inevitability and the power of the triangular *heta-chi*. 'Sometimes the lees are better than the wine'. Or perhaps, it may be even more than that: collecting the strained lees of wine to distill and ferment which takes time and effort, but in the end, a very delicious drink is produced; this is why I named this residence 'grappa'.

ヘタPS
複数の小さな円で三角形
を効率的に食う

ヘタコンセント
隠して隠さず。家具と斜
め壁の隙間の有効利用

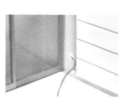

ヘタカーテン溜まり
柔らかいものは三角形に
馴染ませやすい

ヘタ便器
トイレブースのなかで実際に
人が使う空間は三角形に近い

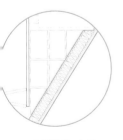

ヘタ収納ボックス
三角形の箱をさまざまに組み
合わせて収納効率を上げるユ
ニバーサル収納→実現せず

ヘタ調味料入れ
さまざまなサイズを持つ調味
料のビン等を組み合わせて
三角形を効率的に食う

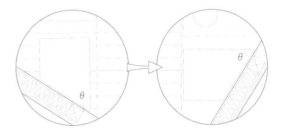

ヘタ収納ワゴン
ヘタ収納がすべて相似形であること
を利用した移動可能な収納ボックス

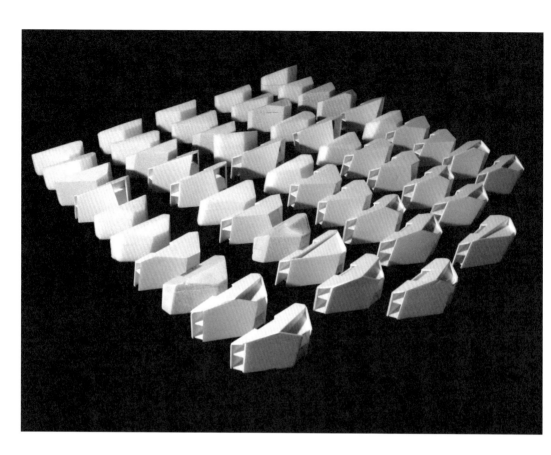

1
2
3
4
5
4
14

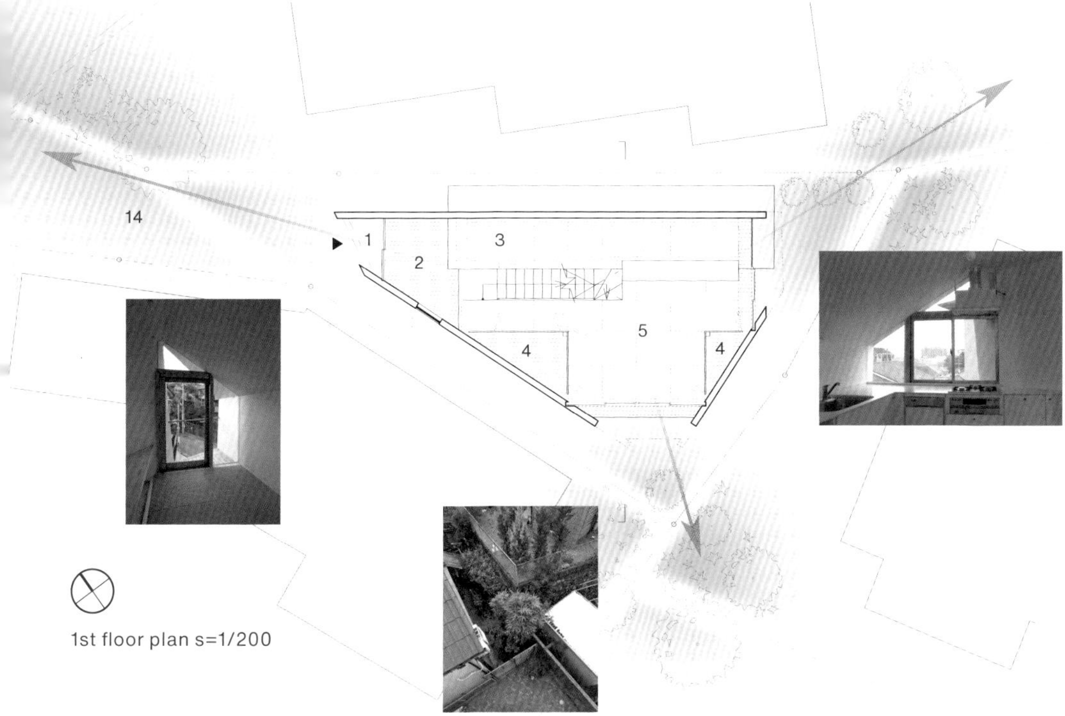

1st floor plan s=1/200

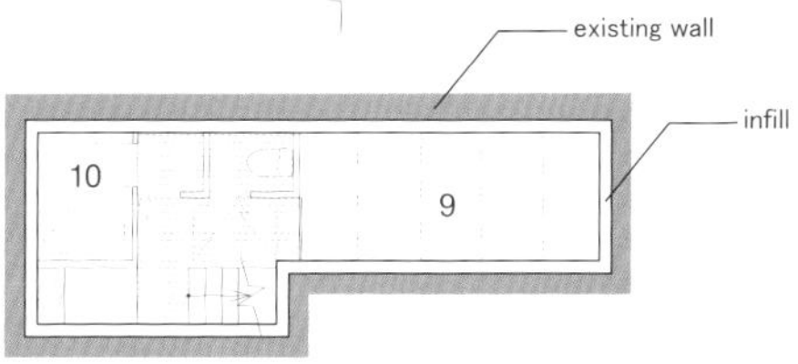

existing wall
infill
10
9

basement floor plan s=1/200

6
9
6
7
4
8
4
6

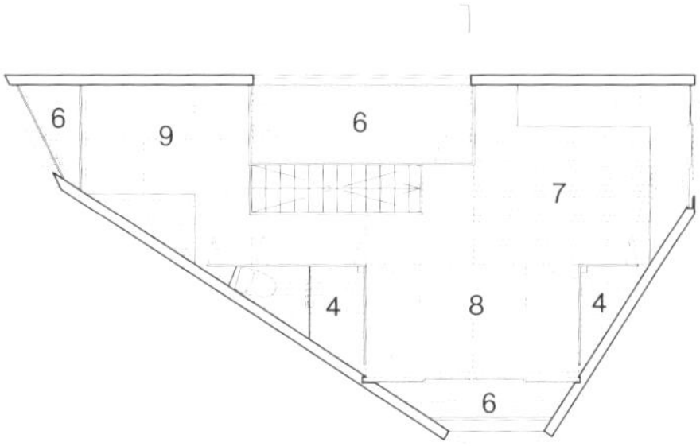

2nd floor plan s=1/200

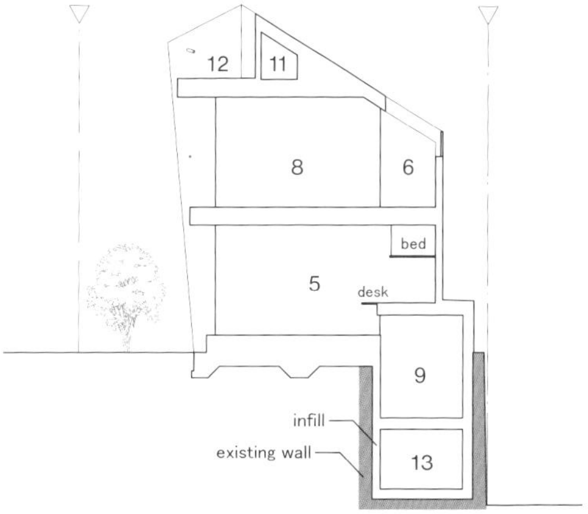

12
11
8
6
bed
5
desk
9
infill
existing wall
13

section s=1/200

1 porch
2 entrance hall
3 study
4 closet
5 children's room
6 terrace
7 dining-kitchen
8 living room
9 bedroom
10 bathroom
11 storage
12 observation platform
13 under floor (storage)
14 parking

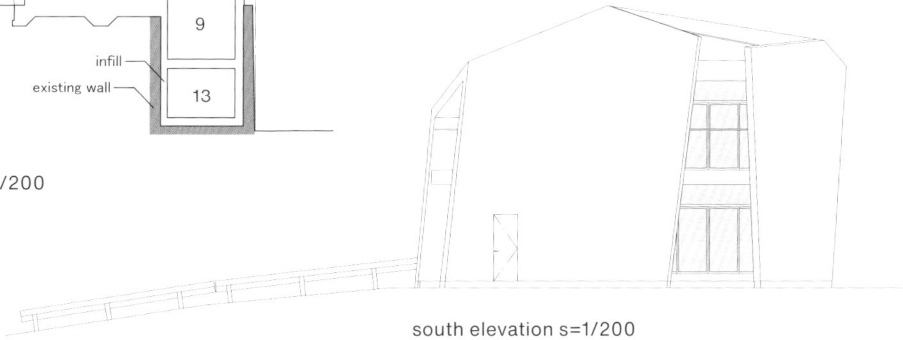

south elevation s=1/200

地盤を掘削し、
空間を自由に造形する。

Excavate the ground and freely shape the space.

クローバーハウス

CLOVER HOUSE

2006

既存の宅造地盤面と石積み擁壁を掘削してできた住宅である。原理的には地盤の掘削によって空間は自由に造形可能である。クローバー型に掘り出された半地下空間に、採光を担うガラスボックスを重ねてできた天井高4.6mのホールが家族共有のスペースであり、その周りに壁の彎曲によってダイニング等のさまざまなスペースがつくり出されている。さらにホールから横穴状に掘られたボックスが、個室や水回りのスペースとなる。構造的には、北側と東側の隣地からの土圧によって発生する建築の滑りに抵抗することが最大の課題であった。9mm厚の鉄板をクローバー型に加工して仕上げ兼用の型枠とし、山留めとの間にコンクリートを充填することで重量を稼ぎ重力式に解決することとした。鉄板は18個のブロックに分割して工場で製作したが、ジョイント部は現場溶接も含めすべて完全溶け込み溶接とすることにより、それ自身が有効な防水層を形成している。

This house was constructed by excavating the existing building's ground surface and masonry retaining wall. In principle, the space can be freely shaped by excavating the ground. The clover-shaped, semi-underground excavated hall, with a ceiling height of 4.6 m and lit by a surrounding glass box, is a space for the family to share. Various spaces, such as the dining room, are created in the hall by bending the walls, while chambers dug horizontally from the hall are spaces for private rooms and wet areas. The biggest structural problem was resisting the slippage of the building caused by the earth pressure from the neighboring land on the north and east sides. 9 mm-thick steel plates were processed into a clover shape, used as both formwork and wall finish, and then concrete was filled between the plates and the retaining wall to gain enough weight to solve the problem. The steel plate was divided into 18 blocks and fabricated at the factory. All joints, including on-site welding, were full penetration welds, making the steel plate an effective waterproofing layer all by itself.

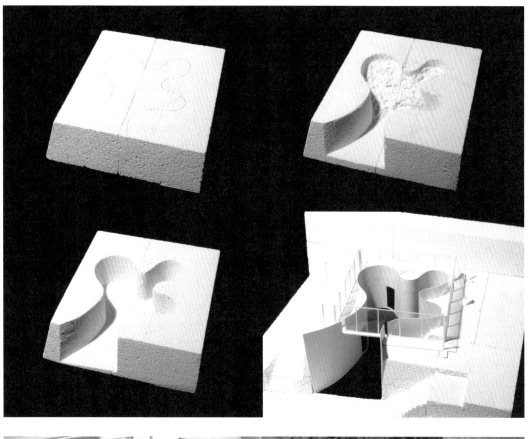

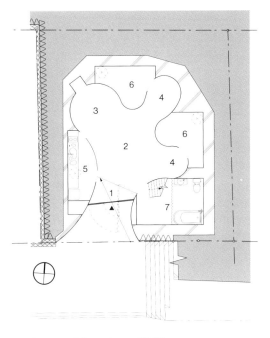

basement floor plan s=1/200

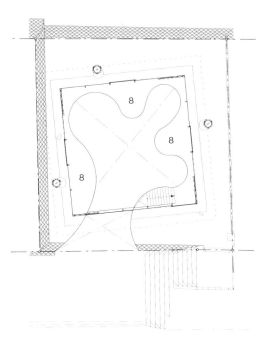

1st floor plan s=1/200

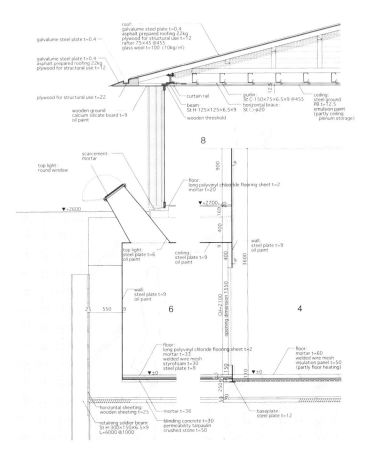

sectional detail s=1/60

1 entry
2 living space
3 dining space
4 children's space
5 kitchen
6 children's room
7 bathroom
8 loft

roof:
galvalume steel plate t=0.4
asphalt prepared roofing 22kg
plywood for structural use t=12
rafter 75×45 @455
glass wool t=100 (10kg/m²)

galvalume steel plate t=0.4

galvalume steel plate t=0.4
asphalt prepared roofing 22kg
plywood for structural use t=12

plywood for structural use t=22

wooden ground
calcium silicate board t=9
oil paint

curtain rail

beam:
St H-125×125×6.5×9
wooden threshold

purlin:
St C-150×75×6.5×9 @455
horizontal brace:
St ○-ϕ20

ceiling:
steel ground
PB t=12.5
emulsion paint
(partly ceiling
plenum storage)

scarcement:
mortar

top light:
round window

top light:
steel plate t=6
oil paint

ceiling:
steel plate t=9
oil paint

floor:
long polyvinyl chloride flooring sheet t=2
mortar t=20

wall:
steel plate t=9
oil paint

wall:
steel plate t=9
oil paint

floor:
long polyvinyl chloride flooring sheet t=2
mortar t=33
welded wire mesh
styrofoam t=30
steel plate t=9

floor:
mortar t=60
welded wire mesh
insulation panel t=50
(partly floor heating)

horizontal sheeting:
wooden sheeting t=25

mortar t=36

retaining soldier beam:
St H-300×150×6.5×9
L=6000 @1000

blinding concrete t=30
permeability tarpaulin
crushed stone t=50

baseplate:
steel plate t=12

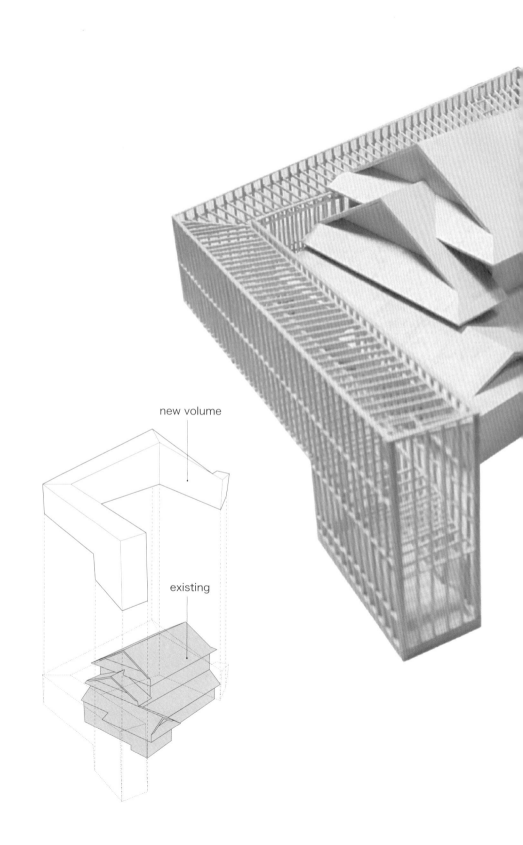

new volume

existing

時間の中の建築。
——繰り返される新旧の「逆転写」。

Architecture in the temporal.
——The repeated "reverse transcription" from the old to the new.

「ハンカイ」ハウス
"HANKAI" HOUSE

2007

東播磨の古い集落の中に建つ古民家のリノベーションである。老朽化に加えて阪神淡路大震災時には「半壊」判定を受けている。そこで特に老朽化や損傷の激しい部分は撤去し、改めて増築によって新たな機能を付加して、家全体として根本的なプログラムの変換を図った。最初に、比較的状態の良好な築90年の母屋部分は残して、老朽化の著しい築300年（と施主はいう）長屋門及び「奥」と呼ばれるエリア、さらに母屋の北側下屋を解体した。そして伝統的な田の字型平面を持つ母屋の周囲に、新たな個室と水回り、スロープを主体とした動線系を配置して、現代住宅へと再生している。面積については4人という家族の成員数に見合うように、むしろ既存の過大な床面積を減築している。構造的には、陶器浩一が開発したツーバイ材を用いた「木造面ラーメン構法」によって構成される新設部分が、母屋に対してとぐろのように巻き付くことで、耐震補強として有効に機能している。

This is a renovation of an old house in an old village in Higashi-Harima, Hyogo Prefecture. In addition to its dilapidated condition, the house was judged to be "half collapsed," *hankai* in Japanese, at the time of the Hanshin-Awaji Great Earthquake. Therefore, we removed the parts of the house that had deteriorated or were severely damaged and added new functions by building an extension, thereby fundamentally transforming the program of the house as a whole. Firstly, the 90-year-old main house, which was in relatively good condition, was left standing, while the 300-year-old (according to the owner) *Nagaya-mon* (gate house) and the area called *Oku* (private section), as well as the northern volume under a lean-to roof, were demolished. The main house, which has a traditional square plan of four rooms in a grid, was then reassembled as a modern residence with new private rooms, wet spaces, and a flow line consisting mainly of a sloping corridor. In terms of floor space, the existing excessive floor area was reduced to accommodate the family of four. The new structure, which is constructed with 2x4-inch series lumber using the "wooden-facing rahmen construction method" developed by Hirokazu Toki, wraps and coils around the main building, effectively reinforcing it against earthquakes.

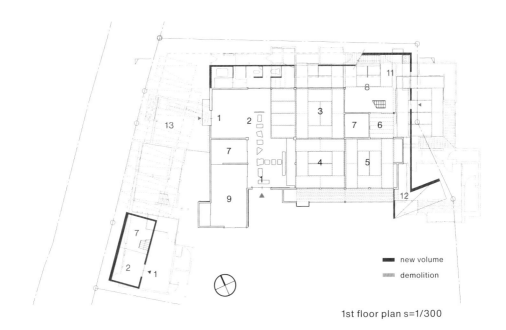

1st floor plan s=1/300

■ new volume

▨ demolition

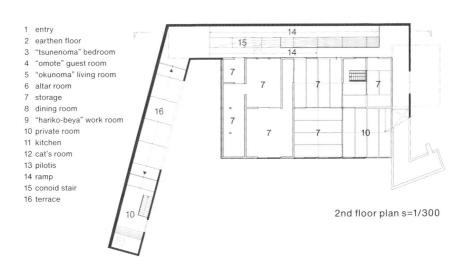

1 entry
2 earthen floor
3 "tsunenoma" bedroom
4 "omote" guest room
5 "okunoma" living room
6 altar room
7 storage
8 dining room
9 "hariko-beya" work room
10 private room
11 kitchen
12 cat's room
13 pilotis
14 ramp
15 conoid stair
16 terrace

2nd floor plan s=1/300

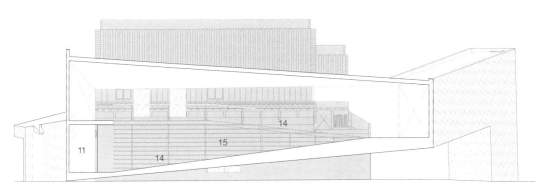

section s=1/200

「庭付き一戸建て
垂直分離二世帯住宅」。

A "vertically separated two-generation family house with a garden."

between

2009

2階レベルに置いた「庭」と呼ぶ屋外スペースを、二世帯住宅で上下からサンドイッチした「庭付き一戸建て住宅」である。2階床スラブまでをRC造で立ち上げ、「庭」を挟んで上空にツーバイ材と構造用合板でつくった木造ボックスを浮かせている。RC基壇は親世帯の住居であり、木造ボックスは子世帯の住居である。2階の僅かな内部空間にはDKが納まっているが、感覚的には「庭」の延長であり土間空間のように使われている。2階床スラブと3階ヴォリュームの水平投影面をずらすことにより、「庭」には多様な場所が生まれた。防球ネットに覆われた「庭」は野球少年のための練習場であり、時には食事スペースともなる。また雨掛かり部分は花壇となり、深い軒下は物干場となる。「庭」を床・壁・天井ともに白く仕上げたのは、上下階ヴォリュームとの図地を反転させ、開放感をより高めることを意図したものであり、水平に大阪湾まで連続する気持ちよいオープンスペースを形づくっている。

This is a detached house with a garden, in which an outdoor space called the "garden" on the second-floor level is sandwiched between the two generation houses, one above the other. RC construction was used from the foundation to the second-floor slab, and a wooden box made of 2x4-inch series lumber and structural plywood floats above the "garden." Inside the RC platform is the residence of the parent family, and the wooden box is the residence of the child family. A small interior space on the second floor houses the DK (Dining and Kitchen), which is an intuitive extension of the "garden" and is used like an earthen floor space. By shifting the horizontal projection of the second-floor slab and the third-floor volume, a variety of places are created in the "garden." The "garden" covered by the netting is often used as a practice area for the grandchildren, who are enthusiastic about baseball, and sometimes as a dining space. The rain-exposed area becomes a flower bed, and the area under the deep eaves becomes a place to hang clothes to dry. The white finish on the floor, walls, and ceiling of the "garden" is intended to enhance the sense of openness by inverting the figure-ground of the upper and lower floor volumes with the "garden" void, creating a spacious open space that extends horizontally towards Osaka Bay.

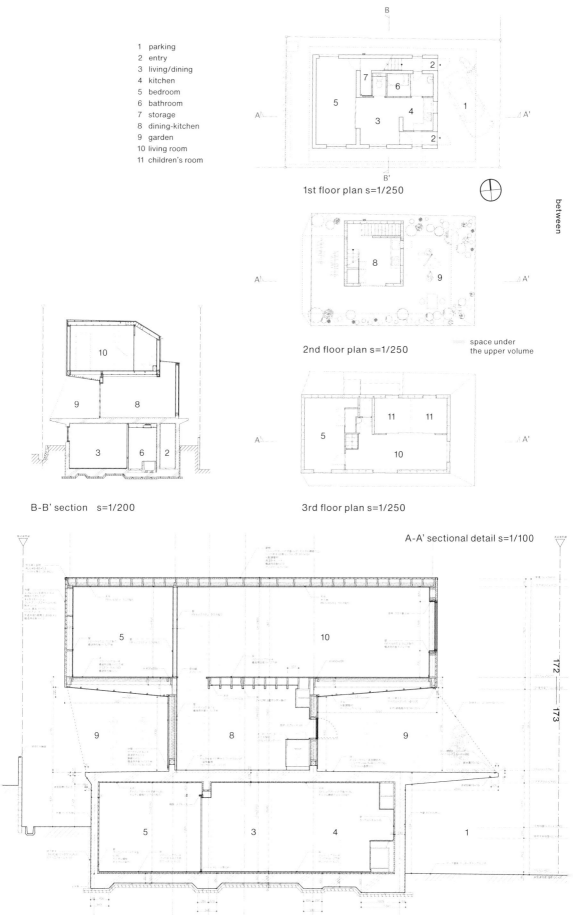

1 parking
2 entry
3 living/dining
4 kitchen
5 bedroom
6 bathroom
7 storage
8 dining-kitchen
9 garden
10 living room
11 children's room

1st floor plan s=1/250

2nd floor plan s=1/250

space under
the upper volume

3rd floor plan s=1/250

B-B' section   s=1/200

A-A' sectional detail s=1/100

between

一挙に解決する
「うねる面格子」。
——透過、遮蔽、装飾、統合。

The "undulating lattices" that resolve all at once.
—— Transmission, shielding, ornament, and integration.

gather
2009

低層高密市街地に建つ木造住宅の増改築プロジェクトである。建ぺい率オーバーという違法状態の解消のため最初に大きく減築して、採光と通風のために３つの坪庭を設けた。次に急な階段を廃止して、吹抜け状の明るい階段室を増築した。そして約1000本、直列に並べると全長2.8kmに及ぶツーバイフォー材で構成する「うねる面格子」によって機能上の問題を一挙に解決することを試みた。面格子は面内・面外の両方向に微妙に傾き、羽根の回転角も変化させながら、室内・室外に関係なく連続して空間をインテグレイトしていく。面格子は単なるデザインに留まらない。同時に耐震補強の目隠しとなり、DKのように室内側に大きく膨らめば、収納としての利用も可能である。道路沿いに塀のように立ち上がった部分では、羽根の角度が異なる面格子がダブルに重なり、通風を確保しながら視線を遮る。それはまた昼には美しいモアレを生じさせ、夜には歩道を柔らかに照らす街路灯ともなっている。

This is an extension and renovation project of a wooden house in a low-rise, high-density urban area. In order to resolve the illegal condition of exceeding building coverage, the house was first largely reduced in size, and three courtyards were added for lighting and ventilation. Next, the existing steep staircase was discontinued, and a new bright stairwell was added. Then, I attempted to solve numerous functional problems at once by using "undulating lattices," consisting of approximately one thousand 2x4-inch pieces of lumber, 2.8 km-long when arranged in a line. The lattice-work tilts slightly in both inward and outward directions and changes the angle of rotation of its blades, continuously integrating the space regardless of whether it is indoors or outdoors. The lattice is more than just a design feature. It also conceals the seismic reinforcement and can be used as a storage space when it expands toward the interior, as it does in the DK (Dining and Kitchen). In the part that rises up along the street like a fence, double-layered lattices with different angles of the blades are used to block the line of sight while introducing a cooling breeze. It also serves as a streetlight that creates a beautiful moiré in the daytime and softly illuminates the sidewalk at night.

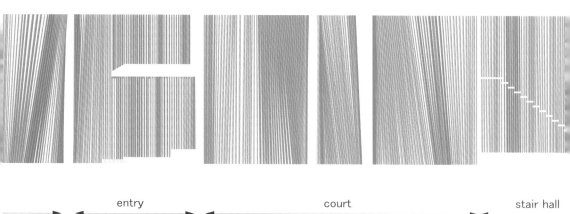

| entry | court | stair hall |

court   stair hall   corridor   gather

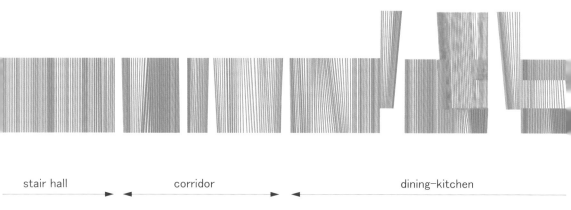

stair hall ►◄ corridor ►◄ dining—kitchen

court |← entry →|

■ demolition

1st floor plan（before）s=1/200

■ renovation

1st floor plan s=1/200

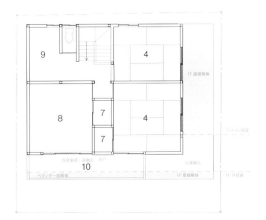

2nd floor plan（before）s=1/200

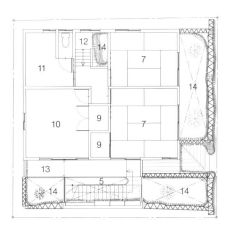

2nd floor plan s=1/200

1	entry	6	bathroom
2	living room	7	closet
3	dining-kitchen	8	bedroom
4	tatami room	9	storage
5	veranda	10	balcony

1	entry	8	bathroom
2	corridor	9	closet
3	dining-kitchen	10	bedroom
4	court	11	storage
5	stair hall	12	study
6	utility room	13	balcony
7	tatami room	14	void

before

after

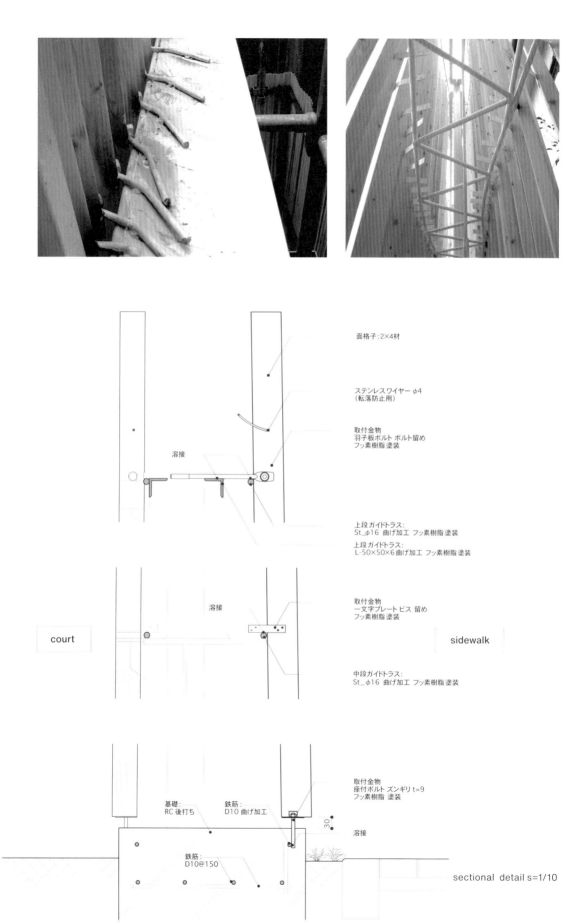

面格子:2×4材

ステンレスワイヤー φ4
(転落防止用)

取付金物
羽子板ボルト ボルト留め
フッ素樹脂 塗装

溶接

上段 ガイドトラス:
St_φ16 曲げ加工 フッ素樹脂 塗装
上段 ガイドトラス:
L-50×50×6 曲げ加工 フッ素樹脂 塗装

取付金物
一文字プレート ビス 留め
フッ素樹脂 塗装

溶接

court

sidewalk

中段ガイドトラス:
St_φ16 曲げ加工 フッ素樹脂 塗装

取付金物
座付ボルト ズンギリ t=9
フッ素樹脂 塗装

基礎:
RC 後打ち

鉄筋:
D10 曲げ加工

30

溶接

鉄筋:
D10@150

sectional detail s=1/10

歴史を超えるインフラ／
時代にうつろうインフィル。

Infrastructure that transcends history,
Infill that changes with the times.

澄心寺庫裏
Chushin-ji Temple Priest's Quarters

2009

庫裏に隣接する客殿は1830年、法堂（はっとう）は1752年の創建である。両堂宇ともに、歴史の中で増改築を重ね、プランは自由に改変されてきた。一方で屋根だけは、銅板へ葺き替えられた以外は不変であった。新しい庫裏の屋根も同様に少なくとも100年は存続し、宗教空間のインフラストラクチャーでありたいと考えた。屋根の非対称性は、境内に対峙する北面、住宅としての南面という対比から導かれたものであるが、構造的にもシェル構造と折板構造を組み合わせて、意匠と構造を合理的に整合させている。同時に落雪処理や動線計画といった機能にも対応している。長寿命化のために、屋根は超硬練りの生コンクリートを用いて施工した。そして大屋根の下に、機能の変化に柔軟に対応する軽快な木造軸組をインフィルとして組み上げている。麓の集落からも見える大屋根がアイコンとなって、地域住民や壇信徒とお寺を繋ぐ役割を担う。ここでは屋根が人々の想いを受け止める「記憶の器」となっている。

The *Kyakuden* reception hall adjacent to the *Kuri* priest's quarters was built in 1830, and the *Hatto* main hall was built in 1752. Both halls have been extended and remodeled throughout their history, and their plans have been freely altered. The roof, however, has remained unchanged except for the copper shingles that have been replaced. The roof of the new priest's quarters was intended to last at least 100 years as well and to be an infrastructure of the religious space. The folded plate combined with shell structure RC roof lends itself to an asymmetrical form that is derived from the contrast between the north side facing the temple grounds and the south side as a residence. At the same time, it also addresses functions such as snowfall control and circulation planning. For longevity, the roof was constructed using ultra-hard-mix fresh concrete. Under the large roof, a light wooden framework that flexibly responds to changes in function is constructed as an infill. The large roof, visible from the village at the foot of the mountain, has become an icon and serves as a link between the temple and local residents and temple members. Here, the roof serves as a "vessel of memory" that receives the thoughts and feelings of the people.

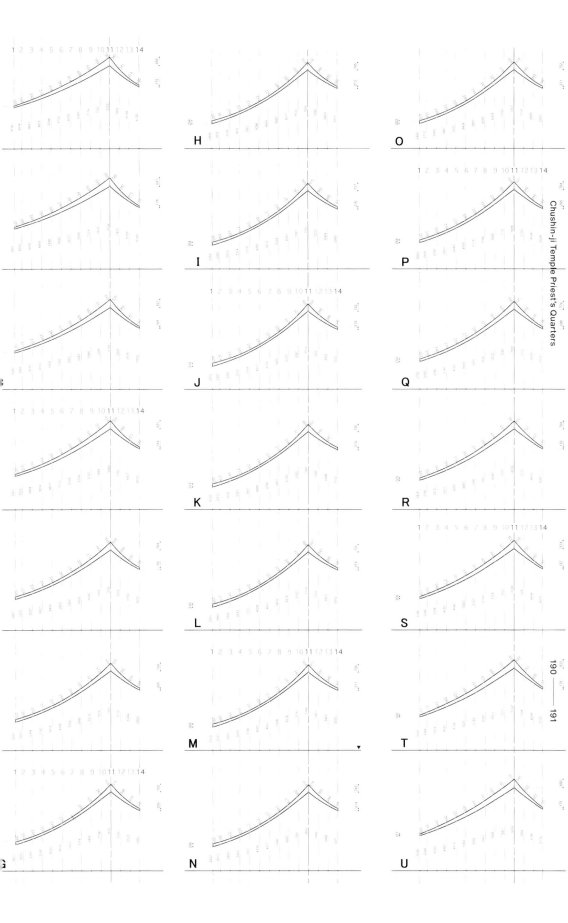

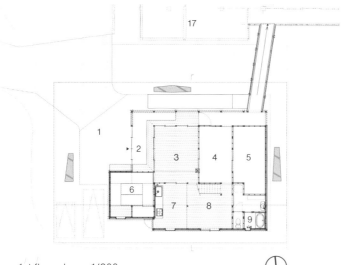

1st floor plan s=1/300

2nd floor plan s=1/300

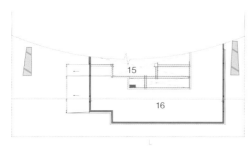

loft floor plan s=1/300

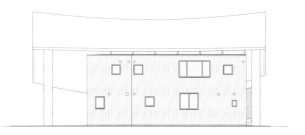

south elevation s=1/300

1 common space (porch
2 entry
3 common space
4 office
5 storage
6 guest room
7 kitchen
8 dining
9 bathroom
10 master bedroom
11 summer room
12 winter room
13 children's room
14 mother's room
15 void
16 loft
17 reception hall

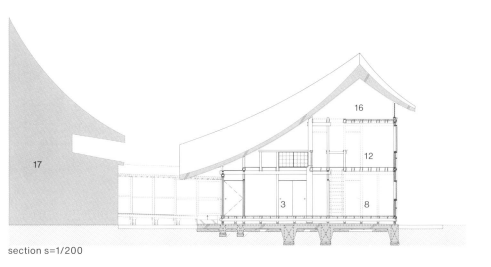

section s=1/200

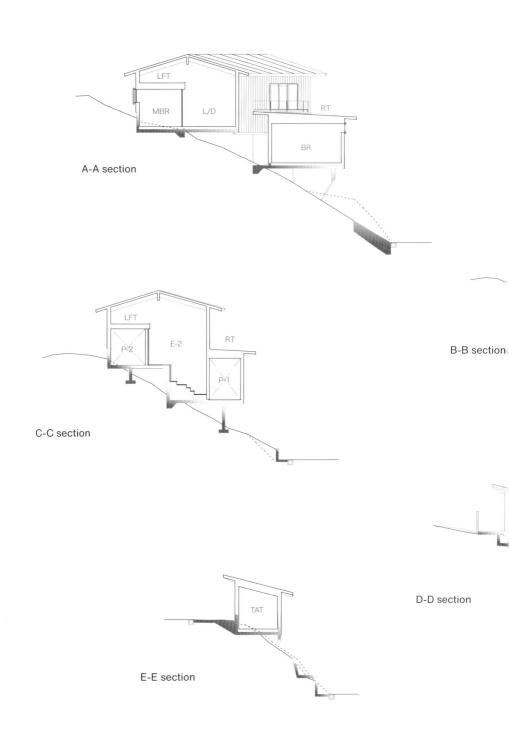

A-A section

C-C section

B-B section

E-E section

D-D section

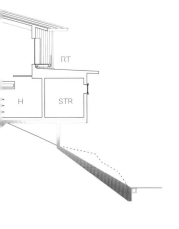

建築と自然を、ソフトに
馴染ませる。──軽インフラと
しての土木の可能性。

Gently adapting architecture to nature.
──The potential of civil engineering as light infrastructure.

bird house
2010

斜面に建築を建てる場合、一般的には擁壁をつくって平場を造成し、そこに後で建築を建てる。つまり土木は建築と自然を橋渡しする役目を担っている。しかしながら、もう少しエレガントに土木と建築の中間くらいの構造物で、建築と自然をソフトに馴染ませる方法はないものだろうか。いわば軽インフラとしての土木の可能性である。この急斜面に建つ住宅は、スカンピ（アカザエビ）のように引っ掛かりの多い軽インフラとしての基礎が斜面をとらえ、その上に安定的に建築を建てることを可能にしている。上下で接道する敷地の特性を利用して、このRC基礎は2つの前面道路を結んで登山道のようなつづら折れのアプローチ動線を提供する。まさにインフラである。そしてヘアピンカーブ状の踊場3ヶ所に「敷地」が発見された。「bird house」という名前は、樹木の枝振りのような基礎の上に、白くて可愛らしい住宅3棟が巣掛けられたような姿から名付けたものである。

When building on a steep site, usually a retaining wall is constructed, and the site is tiered. The earthwork and retaining structure bridge between architecture and nature. However, aren't there other ways for artifice to adapt to nature more gently; a structure that is between earthwork and architecture, something more elegant than a retaining wall? It is the potential of civil engineering as light infrastructure, so to speak. This house is built on a steep slope, and the foundation as a light infrastructure, has many hooks like scampi that grip the slope and allow the building to be stably built on top of it. Taking advantage of the site's unique characteristics, with street access at the top and bottom of the site, the RC foundation connects the two front streets and provides a zigzag approach like a mountain trail. This is what I call "infrastructure." At the landings formed at each turning point of the zigzag ramp, there are three "sites" for structures. The name 'bird house' was given to the three cute white houses nestled on the foundation as if on the branches of a tree.

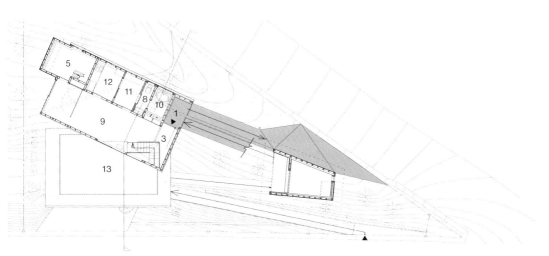

1st floor plan s=1/300

2nd floor plan s=1/300

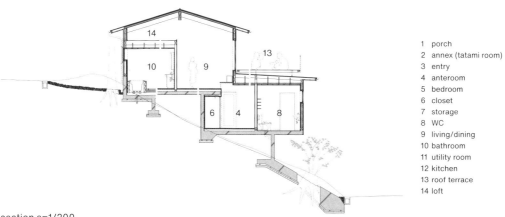

1 porch
2 annex (tatami room)
3 entry
4 anteroom
5 bedroom
6 closet
7 storage
8 WC
9 living/dining
10 bathroom
11 utility room
12 kitchen
13 roof terrace
14 loft

section s=1/200

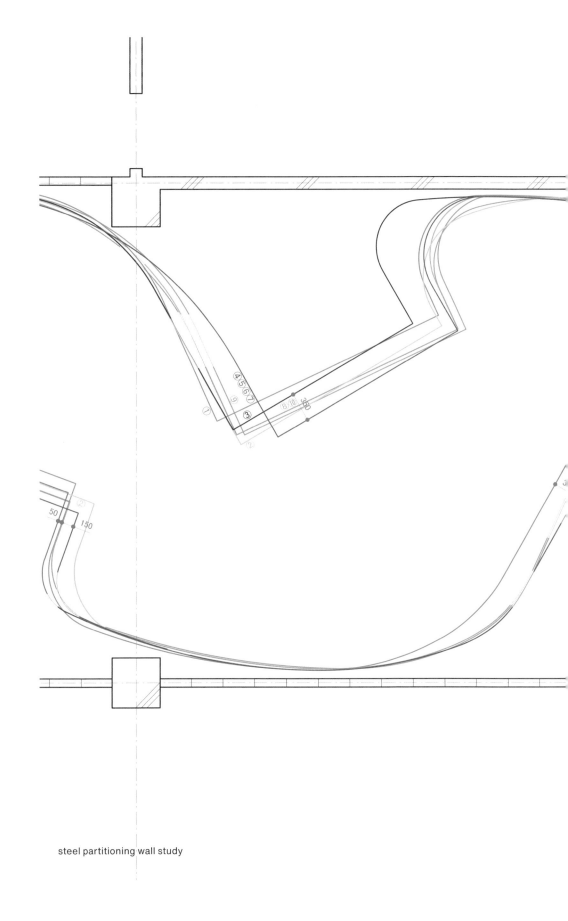

steel partitioning wall study

間仕切壁概念の再定義による「インテリアの打ち放し」。

Redefinition of the partition wall concept
and the "genuine" interior.

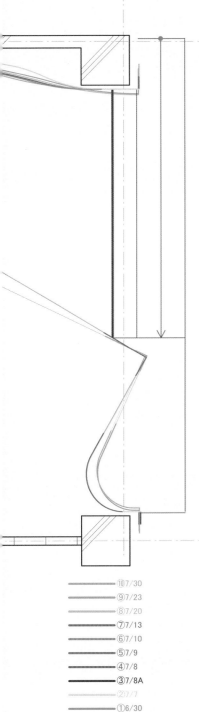

elastico

2010

「仕上げ」という概念について考えてみた。土木とは躯体そのものである。建築は通常、躯体と仕上げから構成されている。一方、インテリアとはほぼ仕上げそのものである。そう考えると「間仕切壁」という中途半端な存在が気持ち悪く感じられた。そこでインテリアを、躯体を欠いた建築として捉え直してみた。すると間仕切壁が躯体を持たない「皮」のように感じられた。つまり骨抜きである。この美容室では、ペラペラの「皮」として、文字通り押せば揺れる2.3mmと4.5mm厚の黒皮鉄板1枚で間仕切壁を形成している。それは純粋なインテリア、つまり「インテリアの打ち放し」と言えないだろうか。街並を引き込むように、鉄板には外壁のレンガタイルの模様を卦書いた。キッチュなレンガ模様が、黒皮特有の鉱物質の鈍い輝きをむしろ際立たせる。全長36mの連続する1枚の鉄板の中に、直角の出隅と曲面が交互に現れて、バロックの曲線の伸びやかさとダブルクリップのような弾力感を生んでいる。

Here, I reconsidered the general idea of "finishes." Architecture is generally composed of a building frame and finishes. On the other hand, it is possible to say that civil engineering is the building frame itself, and the interior is very much the finish. However, once I focused on a part in between them, the partitioning wall left something unexplored, despite being very familiar to us. Then I took the interior to be architecture without a building frame. From this point of view, the partitioning wall could be seen as skin without a skeleton, or in other words, "boneless." I made the partitioning wall of this hair salon with very thin black steel sheet, with a thickness of only 2.3 mm and 4.5 mm, so that it swings softly if you push it. It might be described as a "genuine interior." The black steel has a scratched pattern like brick tiles as if the brick exterior wall is extended inward. Actually, this kitsch surface treatment has emphasized the peculiar dull sheen of black steel. The 36-meters-long continuous steel partition, composed of alternating right-angled protruding corners and curved surfaces, gives rise to elongated Baroque curves with elasticity like a double clip.

⑩7/30
⑨7/23
⑧7/20
⑦7/13
⑥7/10
⑤7/9
④7/8
③7/8A
②7/7
①6/30

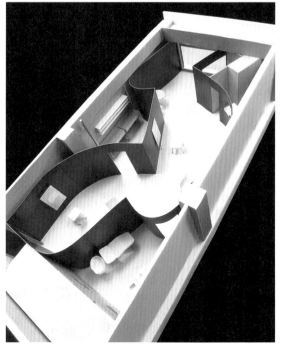

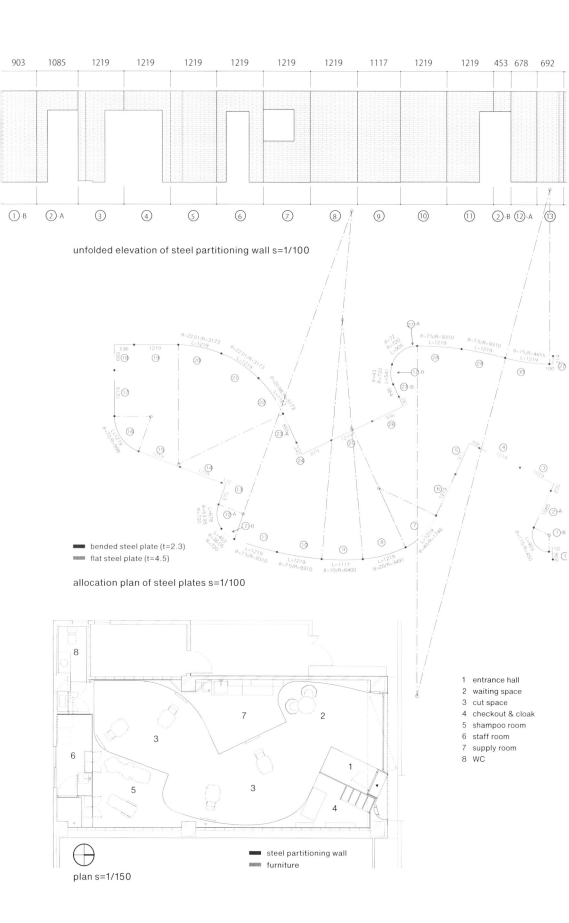

903	1085	1219	1219	1219	1219	1219	1219	1117	1219	1219	453	678	692

① B   ② ·A   ③   ④   ⑤   ⑥   ⑦   ⑧   ⑨   ⑩   ⑪   ②-B ⑫-A   ⑬

unfolded elevation of steel partitioning wall s=1/100

■ bended steel plate (t=2.3)
▬ flat steel plate (t=4.5)

allocation plan of steel plates s=1/100

plan s=1/150

1 entrance hall
2 waiting space
3 cut space
4 checkout & cloak
5 shampoo room
6 staff room
7 supply room
8 WC

■ steel partitioning wall
▬ furniture

1219	1219	1219	1219	1219	1219	1162	453	1219	1219	1219	364	541	905

⑯　　⑰　　⑱　　⑲　　⑳　　㉑　　㉒　　㉓-A　㉔　　㉕　　㉖　　㉓-B ⑫-B ㉒-A

残されたコンクリート基礎を
再生の拠り所にする。

The remaining concrete foundations will be the bases
for revitalization, Part 1.

「元気の種をまく」

Sowing Seeds of Hope

2011

「立ち尽くす」のではなく「座って、見上げる」ことができる
場所をつくりたいと考えた。東日本大震災後何ヶ月か経つ
と瓦礫の撤去も進み、基礎だけが残された光景をあちこち
で見かけるようになった。つらい記憶を宿すコンクリート
の基礎は、しかしそこに建築があり生活があったことを伝
える数少ない証しである。大切に扱いたいと思った。基礎
は形が花壇に似ている。基礎を花壇に見立てて、花を咲か
せようと思いついた。そばには椅子やテーブルも添えて。

I wanted them to find a place where they could rest, and look
up, and not simply stand in silence. Some months after the
Great East Japan Earthquake, removing debris revealed that
only concrete foundations remained throughout the devas-
tated area. The foundations, which hold painful memories,
however, are the few proofs left of the existence of architecture and life in the neighborhood. I felt driven to respect
this. The foundation resembles the shape of a flower bed,
so I came up with the idea to make the foundation look like
a flower bed and let flowers bloom. Chairs and tables would
also be placed next to it.

残されたコンクリート基礎を再生の拠り所にする、その2。

The remaining concrete foundations will be the bases for revitalization, Part 2.

宝来館「星めぐりひろば」

'Hoshimeguri Hiroba': Face of HORAIKAN

2012

旅館宝来館は東日本大震災の津波が3階まで達したものの、鉄骨造4階建ての本館は流失を免れ、震災後は地域の避難所としても機能した。倒壊した木造別館の残されたRC基礎を再利用してつくったのがこのテラスである。宮沢賢治の歌にちなんで女将さんが「星めぐりひろば」と名づけた。美しい砂浜が戻りつつある海岸を望むことができるように、テラスは階段状のウッドデッキになっている。中央にはみんなが集まれるように3m×14mもあるRC造のテーブルを置いた。朝日を浴びながら朝ごはんを食べたり、バーベキューを囲んだり、昼寝をするのにもちょうどよい場所である。イベントの際にはステージとなることもある。本館の回りには白いトレリス（垣根）を巡らせた。工場製作した四角い枠を基礎に蝶番で固定し、クルッと回転させて相互にボルト止めする工法は、人手の確保が難しい被災地での施工に配慮したものであったが、全く無意識に津波を連想させるデザインになっていたことに驚いた。

Although the tsunami from the Great East Japan Earthquake reached the third floor of the Horaikan inn, the four-story steel-framed main building was not swept away and served as a local evacuation center after the disaster. This terrace was built by reusing the remaining RC foundation of the collapsed wooden annex. The landlady of the Horaikan inn named the terrace 'Hoshimeguri Hiroba' after a poem by Kenji Miyazawa. The terrace is a stepped wooden deck with a view of the sandy beach, which is gradually returning to how beautiful it used to be. At the center of the terrace is a 3 m x 14 m-sized RC table where everyone can gather. It is a perfect place to have breakfast under the morning sun, to sit around a BBQ, or to take a nap. It can also be used as a stage for events. A white 'trellis' fence surrounds the main building. The prefabricated square frames were fastened onto the foundation with hinges, rotated, and joined to each other with screws. This method of construction was designed for setting up in the disaster area, where it was difficult to secure skilled workers, but unintentionally, the design turned out to be surprisingly reminiscent of the tsunami.

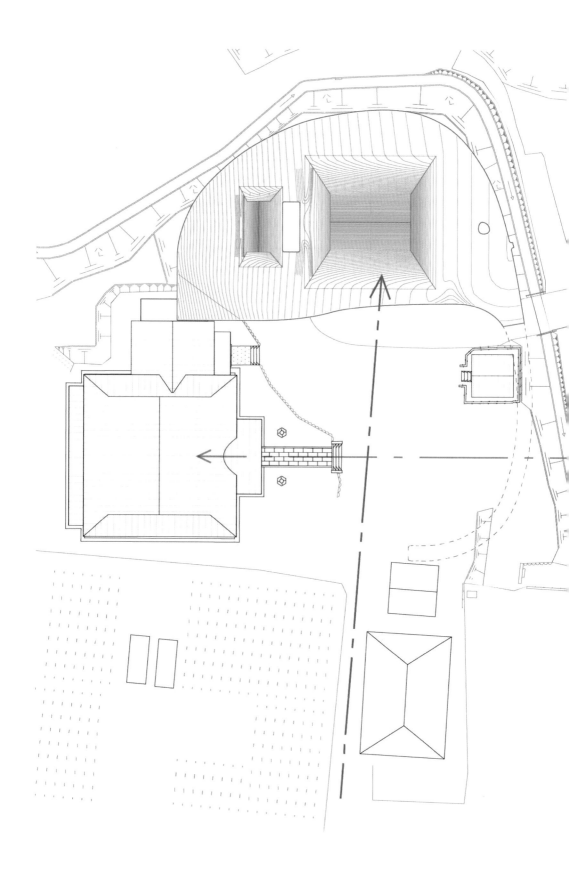

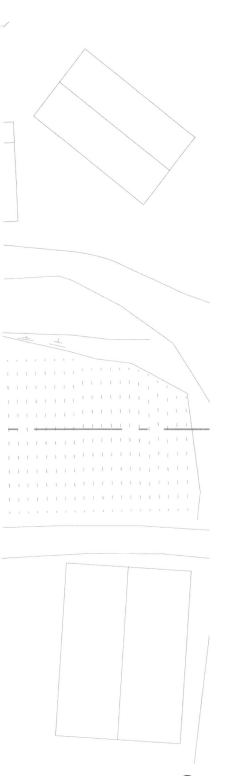

与条件すべてを包み込む、
一枚の大屋根。

A single large roof that encompasses
all design requirements.

真福寺客殿

Shinpuku-ji Temple Reception Hall

2013

旧南参道からの軸線を受け止めて客殿の正面性を強調することで、本堂が建つ東西軸に対して新たに南北軸を整えた。客殿の最も重要な部屋は130名の檀信徒全員が一堂に会する大広間である。用水路に規定されたD型の変形敷地に対して、中央に無柱の大広間に配置し、周辺部に耐震要素ともなる僧侶控室、寺務室等の小部屋群を適宜中庭や坪庭を挟みながら機能的に収めている。外周にはスロープ状の回廊を廻し、本堂や大広間へのバリアフリールートとした。長く延びた縁側は、会合時には玄関の延長として利用されるが、日当りも良く普段は地域に開かれたカフェのように使われることを期待している。RC造の大屋根形状については、当初は緩い片流れ屋根を想定していた。後に檀家総代からの要望に応えて屋根を「摘まみ上げた」ところ、大棟と小棟2つの入母屋が連続したようなフォルムが現れた。大広間上部には大棟の懐を利用して細かい木格子天井を組み、大空間のスケールを調整している。

In contrast to the main temple hall built on the east-west axis, I created the north-south axis by emphasizing the frontal aspect of the new reception hall, which incorporated the axis line from the old southern approach. The most important function of this building is the large hall, which would accommodate 130 parishioners. With an irregular D-shaped site defined by the drain, a large column-free hall is placed at the center; a courtyard and small gardens are interspersed between; while small rooms, such as a waiting room for priests, an administrative office, and others, were built on the periphery, which also serve as earthquake-resistant elements. The external ramp following the D-shaped curve serves as a barrier-free route to the existing main temple hall and the new hall. The long veranda is used as an extension of the entrance for large gatherings of people. Since it is sunny there, I imagine that it will normally function like a cafe that is open to the community. Two hip-and-gable volumes, one big and one small, were "pulled up" from the thin, gently sloped roof. Given the ridges of the hip-and-gable volumes, the RC roof forms a continuous line with the main temple hall. A fine wooden lattice ceiling is constructed, filling in the high ceiling space of the hall to adjust the scale of the large space.

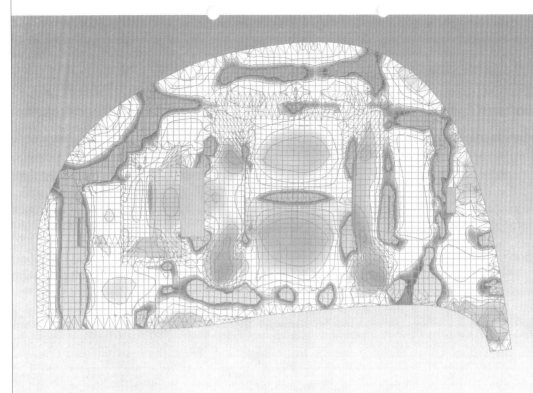

roof moment diagram

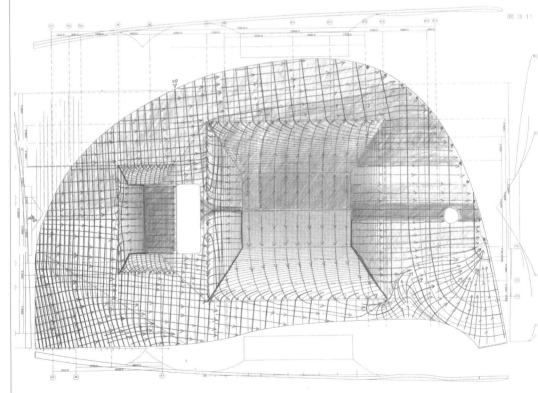

roof drainage plan

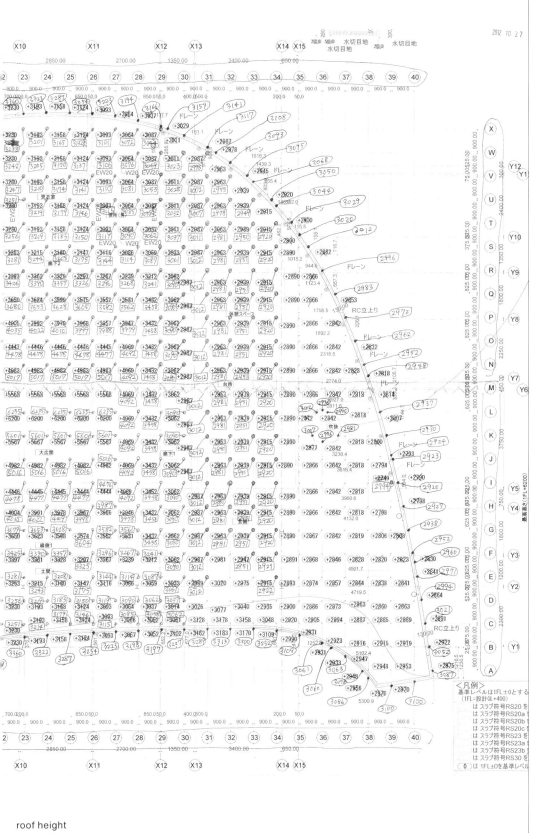

roof height

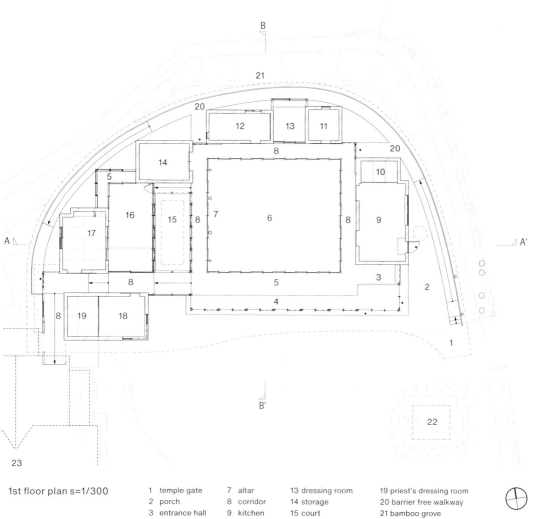

1st floor plan s=1/300

1 temple gate	7 altar	13 dressing room	19 priest's dressing room
2 porch	8 corridor	14 storage	20 barrier free walkway
3 entrance hall	9 kitchen	15 court	21 bamboo grove
4 earthen floor	10 rest space	16 drawing room	22 bell tower
5 veranda	11 WC (m)	17 priest's anteroom	23 main hall
6 reception hall	12 WC (f)	18 office	

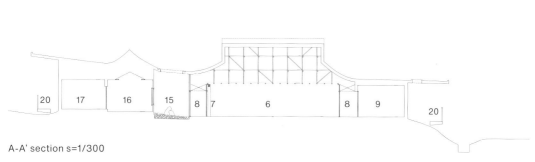

A-A' section s=1/300

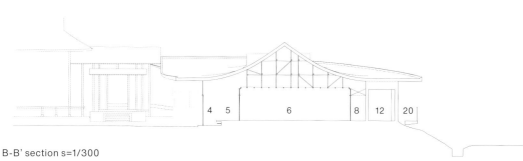

B-B' section s=1/300

真福寺お通夜部屋増築

Shinpuku-ji Temple Reception Hall Extension

2014

客殿の竣工後1年を待たず、小さなお通夜部屋を増築することになった。すでに敷地に余裕がなかったため、客殿の西側に残る小さな三角形の残地に、敷地形状に馴染むようにそら豆型のボリュームを配置することとした。キリスト教会における小聖堂のような位置付けの建築である。お通夜部屋という性格上、近接する木造本堂への延焼を恐れて小規模ながらも構造はRC造としている。本来閉鎖的な用途であり、水平方向に開放的に広がる客殿や伝統的意匠を持つ本堂とのバランスが難しいところであるが、曲面壁を荒い煉瓦積みとしてあえて既存とは異なる表情とすることで伽藍全体としての調和を図っている。

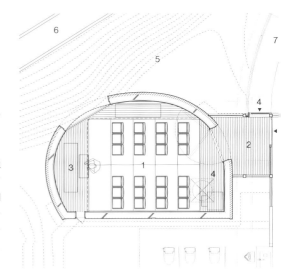

Less than one year after the temple's reception hall was completed, it was decided that a small annex for funeral vigils should be added. Because there was little space left on the site, I designed a small volume with a lima-bean-shaped footprint that fits into a triangular space remaining on the west side of the reception hall. The extension is analogous to a side chapel in a Christian church. Although small in scale, it is built of reinforced concrete to prevent potential fires from spreading to the wooden main hall during vigils when incense or candles burn continuously, sometimes unattended. Though it is fundamentally a closed-off space and it was difficult to balance it against the horizontally expansive reception hall, I sought harmony by covering the curved outer wall of the extension with rough red brick, accentuating the difference in texture and paradoxically achieving balance within the temple complex as a whole.

1 wake room
2 anteroom
3 altar
4 entry
5 bamboo grove
6 drain
7 barrier free
  walkway (existing)
8 corridor (existing)

plan s=1/200

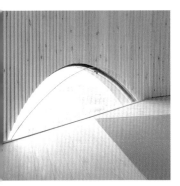

真福寺納骨堂内装工事

Shinpuku-ji Temple Ossuary (Renovation)

2016

客殿新築、お通夜部屋増築に続いて、本堂の一角を改修して納骨堂をつくった。祭壇左側に設けられた達磨棚の背後に位置する小さなスペースである。南からの直射光により朱色に映える空間の中央に、斗栱を載せた素木の独立柱が立つ。お通夜部屋の前で直角に折れた客殿から軸線（＝動線）は、本堂に入ると外陣をなぞるように再度直角に折れ、達磨棚をくり抜いた入口を抜けて独立柱に当たり、三度直角に折れて祭壇背後の位牌堂へと連続していく。

Following the reception hall and addition of the funeral vigil room, a corner in the main hall was renovated to create an ossuary. It is a small space located behind the *daruma* shelf on the left side of the altar. At the center of the space in vermillion, which glows from the direct southern light, stands an independent natural timber column crowned with a *tokyo* (a traditional bracket structure) capital. The axis line (= flow line) from the reception hall, which makes a right-angle turn in front of the vigil room, enters the main hall as if tracing the nave, then turns at a right angle again to encounter the independent column in the ossuary through the opening carved out of the existing *daruma* shelf, at which point a third consecutive right-angle turn finally brings one to the existing mortuary tablet hallway behind the altar.

公共性概念を拡張する。
──自発的な敷地開放が導く歯科医院のかたち。

Extending the concept of publicness.
──The shape of the dental clinic brought by the voluntary opening of the site.

tooth

2013

医院とは本来半公共的な施設であるが、ここでは「自前の公共性」という考え方に基づき、敷地のうち交差点に面する部分をピロティとして開放している。ピロティは駐車スペースであると同時に、周辺住民にとってささやかな近道となり、また雨宿り場所となる。結果的に全体のフォルムが大臼歯に似ることになった。toothというネーミングの由来である。2階に持ち上げた診療スペースは、曲げて強度を増した6mm厚鋼板を構造体として用いて、ワンルームを流動的に間仕切っている。四周を巡るテラスはステンレスメッシュで覆われており、診療スペースに対するバッファーとなって外部からの視線や日照を柔らかく遮り、内部空間に広がりを与える。コーナーに設けた3つの診療室は、いずれもユニット台を開放的なコーナーウィンドウに向かって配置していることが特徴であり、さらに天井高、テラスの奥行、日照などとの関係によってそれぞれ微妙に異なる雰囲気を持つようにデザインしている。

Dental clinics have traditionally been semi-public facilities, but in this case, based on the notion of "voluntary communality," I created the large open 'pilotis' facing the intersection. The overall form coincidentally came to resemble a molar. This is why the project is named 'tooth'. Though 'pilotis' are often used for parking areas, I anticipate that the space will also at times serve as a shortcut for pedestrians and that the clinic will be a comfortable place where local residents can take shelter from the rain. The one-room space on the second-floor treatment area is fluidly partitioned with a structure made out of 6mm-thick steel plates, curved to provide additional strength. The terrace on the periphery is a semi-outdoor space covered with stainless-steel mesh, serving as a buffer that softly deflects the view from outside and sunlight from entering the treatment area while simultaneously imbuing the interior with an expansive quality. The three consultation and treatment rooms, situated at the corners, were each designed to have a subtly different atmosphere by varying the height of the ceiling, depth of the terrace, and amount of sunlight. The dental chair units are all arranged to face an open corner window.

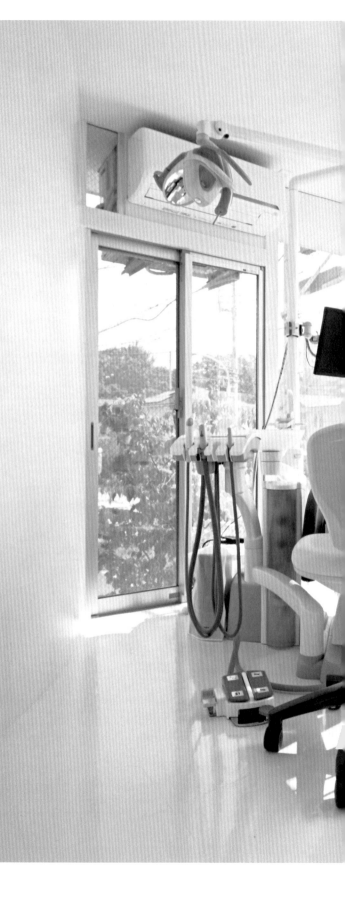

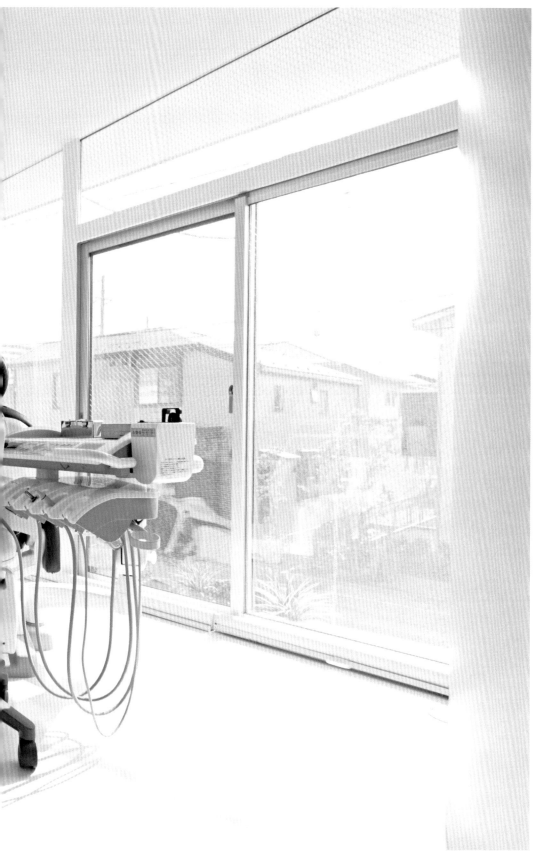

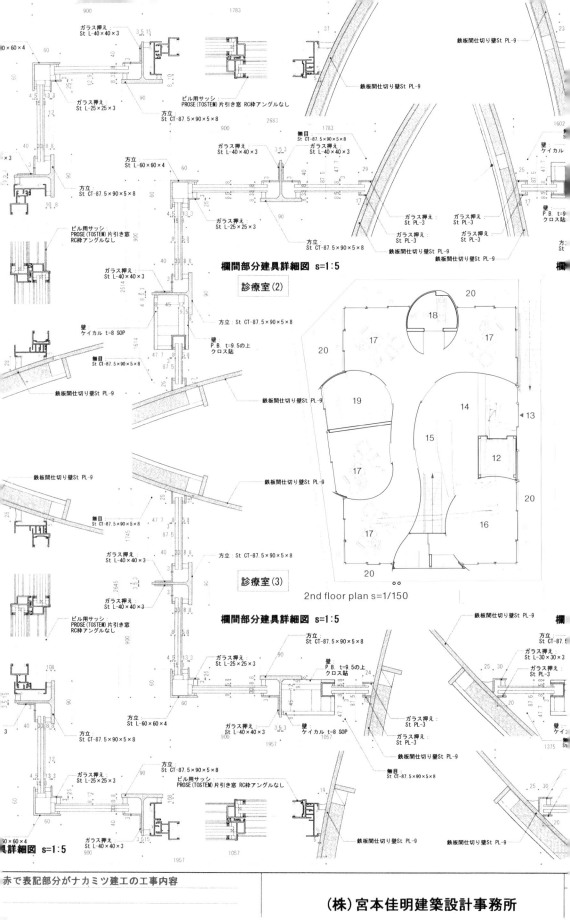

ガラス押え
St L-40×40×3

3.5 15

60×60×4

方立
St CT-87.5×90×5×8

ガラス押え
St L-25×25×3

鉄板間仕切り壁 St PL-9

鉄板間仕切り壁 St PL-9

ビル用サッシ
PROSE(TOSTEM) 片引き窓 RC枠アングルなし

方立
St CT-87.5×90×5×8

方立
St L-60×60×4

ガラス押え
St L-40×40×3

3.5 3

ガラス押え
St L-40×40×3

無目
St CT-87.5×90×5×8

壁
ケイカル

ビル用サッシ
PROSE(TOSTEM) 片引き窓
RC枠アングルなし

ガラス押え
St L-25×25×3

方立
St CT-87.5×90×5×8

ガラス押え
St PL-3

ガラス押え
St PL-3

ガラス押え
St PL-3

ガラス押え
St PL-3

壁
P.B. t=9.5
クロス貼

鉄板間仕切り壁St PL-9

鉄板間仕切り壁St PL-9

欄間部分建具詳細図 s=1:5

診療室(2)

ガラス押え
St L-40×40×3

方立 St CT-87.5×90×5×8

壁
ケイカル t=8 SOP

無目
St CT-87.5×90×5×8

鉄板間仕切り壁St PL-9

20

18

17

17

20

19

14

17

15

13

12

17

16

20

20

20

2nd floor plan s=1/150

鉄板間仕切り壁 St PL-9

鉄板間仕切り壁 St PL-9

無目
St CT-87.5×90×5×8

ガラス押え
St L-40×40×3

ビル用サッシ
PROSE(TOSTEM) 片引き窓
RC枠アングルなし

方立: St CT-87.5×90×5×8

ガラス押え
St L-40×40×3

診療室(3)

欄間部分建具詳細図 s=1:5

方立
St CT-87.5×90×5×8

ガラス押え
St L-25×25×3

壁
P.B. t=9.5の上
クロス貼

鉄板間仕切り壁St PL-9

方立
St CT-87.5

ガラス押え
St L-30×30×3

ガラス押え
St PL-3

方立
St L-60×60×4

方立
St CT-87.5×90×5×8

ガラス押え
St L-40×40×3

壁
ケイカル t=8 SOP

ガラス押え
St PL-3

鉄板間仕切り壁St PL-9

壁
ケイ

方立
St CT-87.5×90×5×8

ビル用サッシ
PROSE(TOSTEM) 片引き窓 RC枠アングルなし

無目
St CT-87.5×90×5×8

ガラス押え
St L-25×25×3

60×60×4

ガラス押え
St L-40×40×3

鉄板間仕切り壁St PL-9

鉄板間仕切り壁St PL-9

具詳細図 s=1:5

赤で表記部分がナカミツ建工の工事内容

（株）宮本佳明建築設計事務所

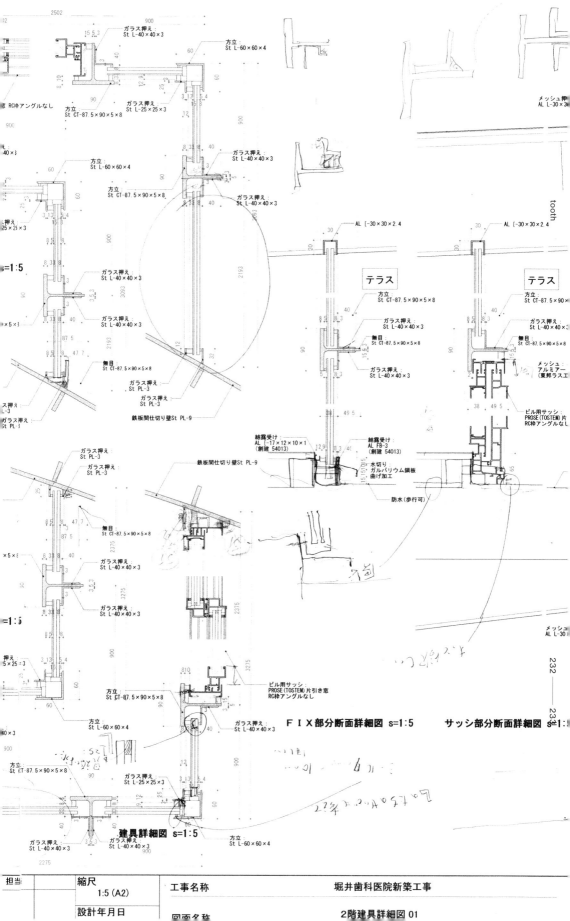

ガラス押え
St L-40×40×3

方立
St L-60×60×4

ガラス押え
St CT-87.5×90×5×8

ガラス押え
St L-25×25×3

RC枠アングルなし

メッシュ押
AL L-30×3

方立
St L-60×60×4

方立
St CT-87.5×90×5×8

ガラス押え
St L-40×40×3

ガラス押え
St L-40×40×3

tooth

AL [-30×30×2.4

AL [-30×30×2.4

テラス

テラス

方立
St CT-87.5×90×5×8

方立
St CT-87.5×90×5×

=1:5

ガラス押え
St L-40×40×3

無目
St CT-87.5×90×5×8

ガラス押え
St L-40×40×3

ガラス押え
St L-40×40×3

無目
St CT-87.5×90×5×

メッシュ：
アルミアー
(東邦ラスエ

ガラス押え
St L-40×40×3

無目
St CT-87.5×90×5×8

ガラス押え
St PL-3

ガラス押え
St PL-3

鉄板間仕切り壁St PL-9

ビル用サッシ：
PROSE (TOSTEM) 片
RC枠アングルなし

ガラス押え
St PL-3

結露受け
AL [-17×12×10×1
(創建 54013)

結露受け
AL FB-3
(創建 54013)

ガラス押え
St PL-3

水切り
ガルバリウム鋼板
曲げ加工

鉄板間仕切り壁St PL-9

無目
St CT-87.5×90×5×8

防水(歩行可)

メッシュ
AL L-

ガラス押え
St L-40×40×3

ガラス押え
St L-40×40×3

=1:5

ビル用サッシ：
PROSE (TOSTEM) 片引き窓
RC枠アングルなし

方立
St CT-87.5×90×5×8

ガラス押え
St L-40×40×3

FIX部分断面詳細図 s=1:5

サッシ部分断面詳細図 s=1:

方立
St L-60×60×4

方立
St CT-87.5×90×5×8

ガラス押え
St L-25×25×3

建具詳細図 s=1:5

ガラス押え
St L-40×40×3

ガラス押え
St L-40×40×3

方立
St L-60×60×4

担当		縮尺	1:5 (A2)	工事名称	堀井歯科医院新築工事
		設計年月日		図面名称	2階建具詳細図 01

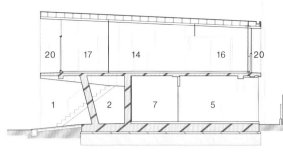

section s=1/200

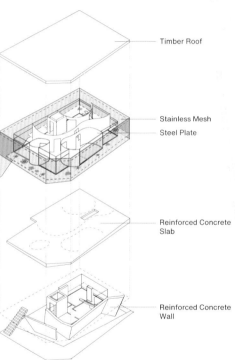

Timber Roof

Stainless Mesh
Steel Plate

Reinforced Concrete
Slab

Reinforced Concrete
Wall

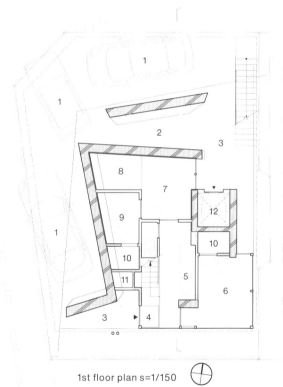

1st floor plan s=1/150

1	parking	11	PS
2	bicycle parking	12	EV
3	porch	13	entry
4	service entry	14	entrance hall
5	kitchenette	15	reception
6	director's room	16	waiting room
7	staff room	17	treatment room
8	dressing space	18	x-ray
9	storage	19	preparation room
10	mechanical	20	terrace

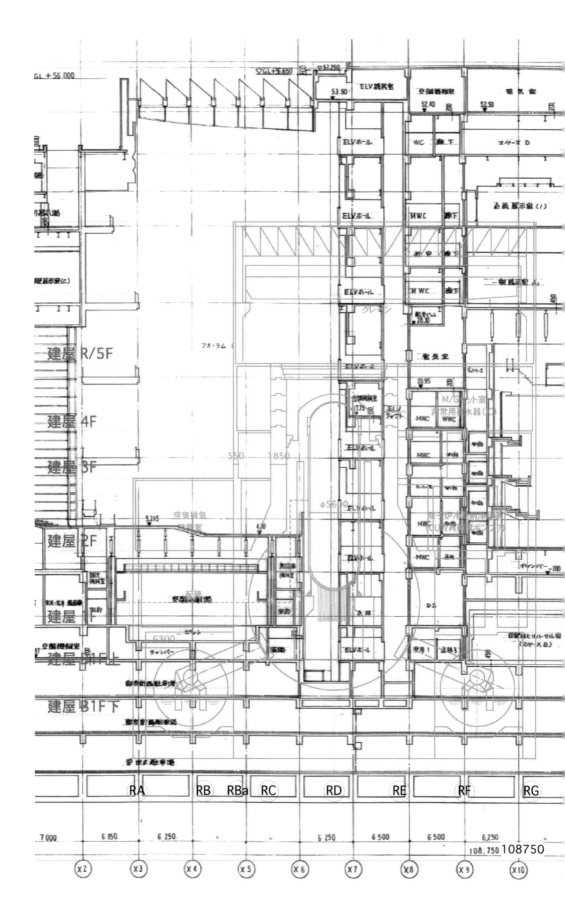

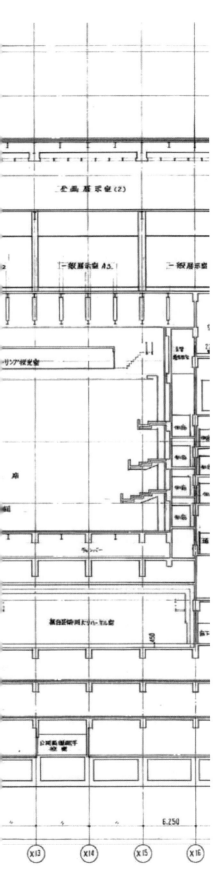

原子炉建屋を
原寸大でトレースする。

Trace the reactor building at 1:1 scale.

福島第一さかえ原発
Fukushima Dai-ichi Sakae Nuclear Plant

2013

あいちトリエンナーレ2013への出品作品。メイン会場となる愛知芸術文化センターの床、壁、天井に、福島第一原発のうちBRW-4型原子炉を内蔵する2～4号機の原寸断面図をラインテープで描いた。テープの総延長は8kmに及ぶ。名古屋の繁華街である栄という立地と会場の巨大スケールが、観客に原発を原寸で感じてもらうというアイデアを喚起させた。クランク状の断面で2階レベルにおいて連続するふたつの巨大な吹抜けに、各階がバルコニー状に張り出すという芸術文化センターならではの空間構成が、巨大な図面を統合的に感得できる絶妙な視点場を提供してくれる。建築の生産現場では、原寸場と呼ばれる体育館のような場所で、床に文字通り原寸図面を描いて鉄骨部材等の納まりを検討することがある。ヴァーチャルな図面が物に転じ、図面に命が宿る場所である。このプロジェクトにおいて、芸文センターは原発のための唯一無二の原寸場として見出されたのかもしれない。

This is a work to be exhibited in Aichi Triennale 2013. The floor, walls, and ceiling of the Aichi Arts Center, the main venue of the Triennale, were covered with line tape depicting a full-scale cross-sectional view of Fukushima Daiichi Nuclear Power Plant Units 2-4, which contained the BRW-4 nuclear reactor. The total length of the tape is 8 km. It was the massive scale of the venue and the location of Sakae, a downtown area in Nagoya, that inspired me to transfer the outlines of the reactor building in its actual size. The unique interior layout of the venue, with its two large atriums linked in a crank-like formation and each floor extending out into space like a balcony, provides an ideal viewpoint from which to take in the overall cross-sectional view of the reactor building, marked out in tape. At architectural production sites, 1:1 blueprints of the proposed structure are drawn on the floor of a gymnasium-like space to consider how steel frames and other materials will fit. This is where a virtual blueprint gains physical substance and comes to life. For this project, the Aichi Arts Center was perhaps the only space that could have housed a full-scale blueprint of the nuclear power plant.

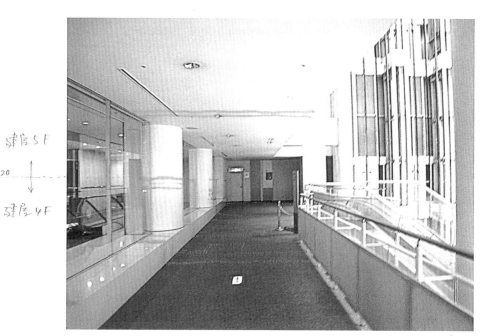

建屋5F

タセンター
EL+1620

建屋4F

格納容器の天端が表れる。
6FL+1620の化粧.

CH=2900.

6F

img-6019.

建屋5F

建屋4F

格納容器の天端が表れる

CH=2900, エレベータホールまわり.

6F

img-6024

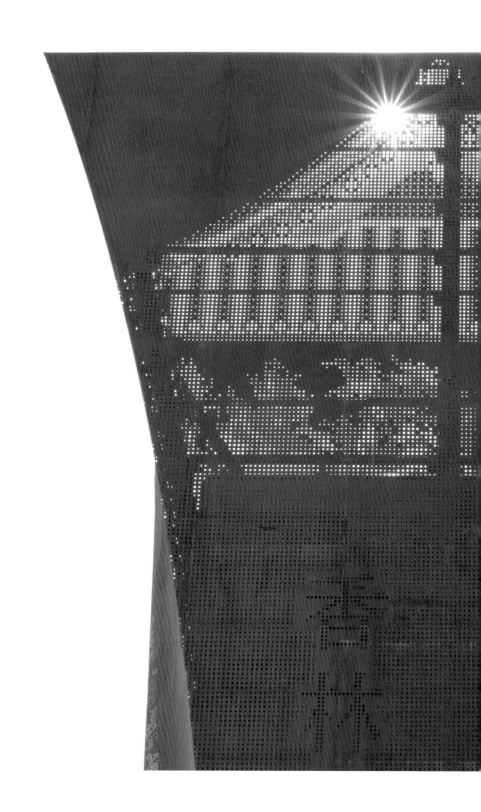

鉄板一枚でつくる 「厚みのない山門」。

A "temple gate without thickness"
made from a single sheet of steel plate.

香林寺ファサード改修
Korin-ji Temple Façade Renovation
2015

旧甲州街道に面した鰻の寝床状の敷地に建つ都市型寺院に、お寺の顔となる看板建築的ファサードを付加するプロジェクトである。限られた敷地の中で、鉄板一枚にさまざまな想いを込めて「厚みのない山門」をつくった。2.3mm厚のコールテン鋼板に、入母屋屋根、唐破風、寺紋、宗紋、元寺のシンボルである大銀杏、花頭窓、灯篭といった文様をパンチング加工して、格式と重厚さに加えて親しみやすさも合わせ持つ外観とした。「山門」の設置により、元々奥深い敷地はより深くなり、本堂に至る長い動線を「参道」としてデザインし直すことが可能になった。面一に納まった山門の可動部は内側に大きく観音開きとすることが可能で、出棺時に近隣からの視線を気にすることなく、円滑な動線を確保している。3次元に湾曲した山門は、街路に向かって大きく庇状に張り出し、雨宿りのできるポケットパークを提供し、夜には行灯のように歩道を照らして、お寺としての公共的な役割を果たしている。

This design adds a dynamic new façade to the front of a temple built on a narrow yet deep "eel's nest" plot of land typical of urban areas. A virtually two-dimensional temple gate is created from a single surface of steel plate, making efficient use of the site's limited space. A pattern graphically conveying the temple's essence with elements like an undulating *karahafu* gate top, sacred emblem, gingko trees, and curvilinear *katomado* windows is punched into 2.3 mm-thick COR-TEN weathering steel, creating a high-impact yet friendly and approachable temple façade for an urban environment. With the addition of the new "temple gate" at the front, the already deep site becomes even deeper, and the path from the gate to the main temple hall is elongated to evoke a pilgrimage route. The façade has a dramatic overhang, curving outward over the sidewalk, with the space beneath the eaves acting as a pocket park for residents, and the light from the temple illuminating its surroundings acts like a paper-shade lantern at night.

sectional detail s=1/60

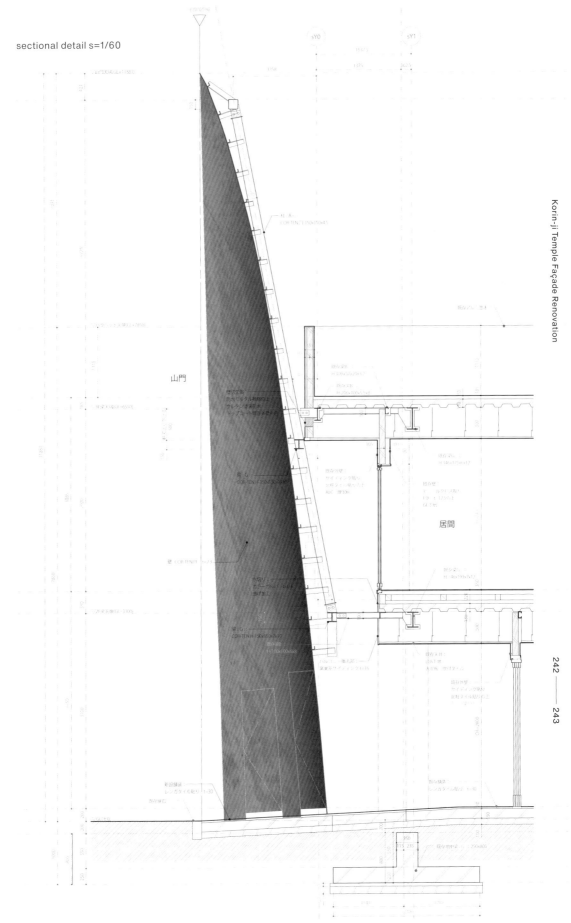

山門

居間

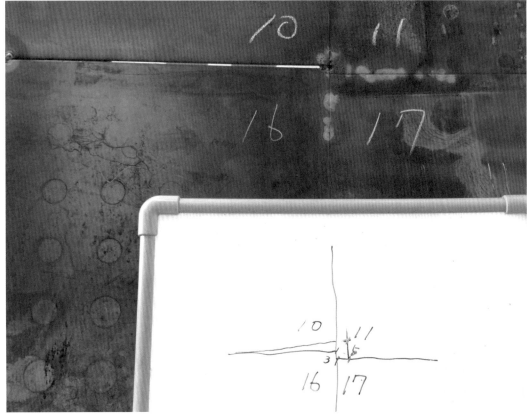

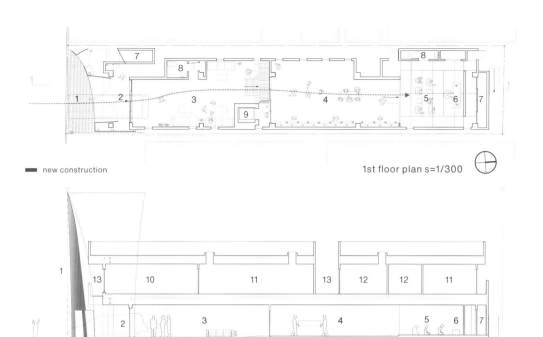

new construction

1st floor plan s=1/300

section s=1/300

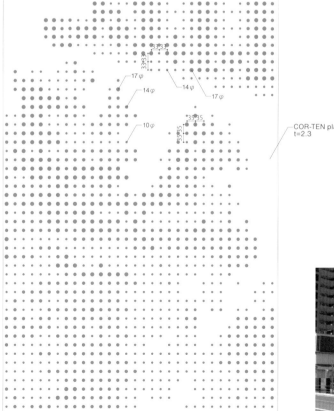

1 temple gate
2 entry
3 lobby
4 ossuary way
5 hall
6 altar
7 storage
8 WC
9 EV
10 waiting room
11 corridor
12 bedroom
13 terrace

COR-TEN plate
t=2.3

perforated panel detail s=1/15

before

香林寺改修 II 期──タカラブネ

Korin-ji Temple Renovation II
── SEVEN GODS' GARDEN

completion undecided

第 II 期工事として、元は中華料理店の社員寮であった２階を改修して、庫裏へとコンバージョンする計画である。旧甲州街道に面したリビングルームは葬儀や法事の際には控室ともなる。リビングルームの背後に中庭を挟みながら５つの個室と２つの水回りを並べている。個室はそれぞれ、ペントハウス状に飛び出した大きなハイサイドライトと屋上への専用階段を持つ。また床に開閉可能なインナートップライトを設けることによって、個室自体が1階本堂に光と風を導く環境調整装置としても機能する。ペントハウス群は屋上に挿入された"blade"と呼ぶ曲面により構成されている。"blade"は高層マンションからの見下ろしや富士山への眺望等に対応して異なるデザインを持ち、ファサードと同様に七福神の図像をパンチングで刻印したコールテン鋼板で仕上げる予定である。

This project is the second phase planned for Korin-ji Temple. In the second phase, the second floor, which was originally used as a Chinese restaurant's dormitory, will be drastically renovated into a priest's living quarter. A spacious living room, facing Koushu Road, is also planned for Buddhist memorial services. Behind the living room, five private rooms and two wet areas are aligned facing across a courtyard, so as to match the deep site form. Each private room has a large clearstory that sticks out like a penthouse on the rooftop, with an exclusive staircase to the rooftop. Additionally, an openable inner top light installed on the floor allows each private room to function as a device for adjusting the environment in the main hall on the first floor by directing light and wind as necessary. Penthouses are composed of "blade" with curving surfaces, each with slightly different designs, responding to the surrounding settings, such as views looking down from the adjacent high-rise apartment or a view to Mt. Fuji. "Blade" is to be finished with punch-holed COR-TEN steel with icons that match the façade. The scenery of penthouses sitting close together on the narrow and long rooftop invokes the image of *Shichifukujin* (Seven Gods of Fortune) on a treasure ship.

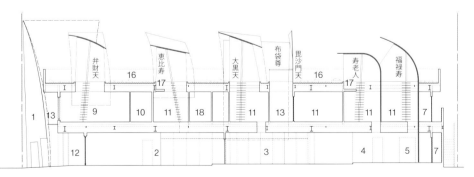

section s=1/300

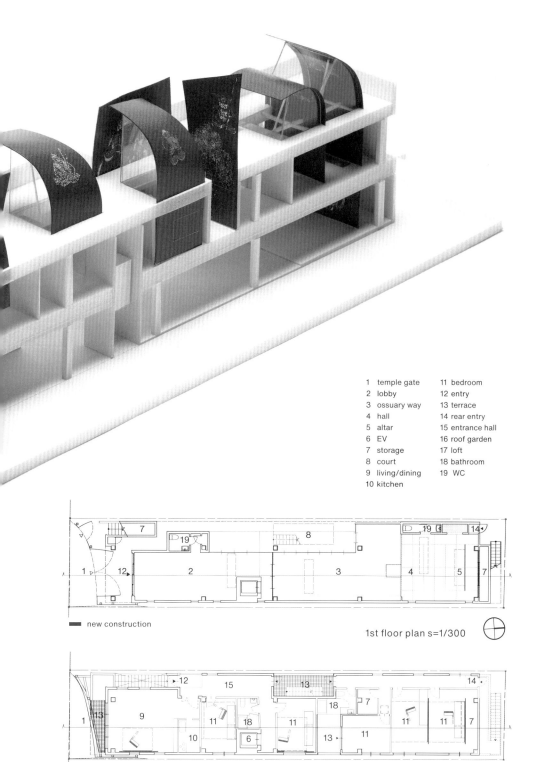

1 temple gate	11 bedroom
2 lobby	12 entry
3 ossuary way	13 terrace
4 hall	14 rear entry
5 altar	15 entrance hall
6 EV	16 roof garden
7 storage	17 loft
8 court	18 bathroom
9 living/dining	19 WC
10 kitchen	

new construction

1st floor plan s=1/300

2nd floor plan s=1/300

仮設団地に「傘」を差し掛ける。

An "umbrella" is held over the temporary housing complex.

御船町甘木・玉虫仮設団地
みんなの家

Home-For-All in Amagi and Tamamushi

2017

熊本地震の被災地に計画された「みんなの家」。常設型としてRC基礎を持つ。大きな軒下と四周を巡る広い縁側を持ち、住民の皆さんが気軽に立ち寄って座ることができる。切妻の勾配を強くして軒を低く保ち、屋根を一本足の棟持ち柱で支えることで、親しみやすい「傘の字」を仮設団地に差し掛けている。小さな室内空間を包む外壁は、周辺の風景になじむ左官仕上げとした。遠くに熊本市街地を望む公園の端に建つ玉虫のみんなの家では、深い藍色の掻き落とし、甘木では艶やかな朱色の土佐漆喰の磨きとしている。甘木仮設団地が建つ民有地にあった母屋は地震後に解体されたが、その記憶を伝えるために基礎石を再利用して擁壁をつくり、古瓦を木端建てで積んで階段を設けた。階段は道路を挟んだお寺の軸線を受け止め、まるで山門のように参道にポーチを差し掛けている。「傘」を中心にして、お寺に隣接する消防屯所とともに、周辺が小さなシビックセンターのように感じられる。

These are two 'Home-For-All' projects planned in the area affected by the Kumamoto earthquake. These are built permanently and sit on RC foundation. The main features are the deep eaves and wide veranda on all four sides, which affords residents a place to stop and sit. The gabled roof pitch is steep to lower the eaves and is supported by an independent column at the ridge, giving the impression of the familiar character of the umbrella, 傘, sheltering the temporary housing complex. The exterior walls enveloping the minimal interior space were finished with plaster to fit in with the landscape. In Tamamushi, it stands in the corner of a park overlooking the city of Kumamoto in the distance, so a deep navy-blue plaster with an uneven scraped finish was chosen. In contrast, in Amagi, it has a glossy vermilion plaster finish. The Amagi temporary housing complex is built on privately owned land. The owner's house was demolished after the earthquake, but in order to convey that memory, the foundation stones were reused to create a retaining wall, and old roof tiles were stacked together to create stairs. The stairs catch the axis of the temple from across the road, and the porch acts as a temple gate, sheltering the approach. With the "umbrella" at the center and the fire station neighboring the temple, the surrounding area feels like a small civic center.

セルフビルドの継承 ——新旧素材の対比が生む、 新しい風景。

Inheritance of self-building
—— New scenery created by the contrast of old and new materials.

こまめ塾
Komame Commons

2019

クライアントの父親が自ら積み上げた補強コンクリートブロック（CB）造のりんご園監視小屋に、本格的な耐震補強を施して、学習塾、託老所、生活クラブ生協のステーション等の複合機能を持ったコモンスペースへとコンバージョンするプロジェクトである。家族の記憶が宿る既存の躯体や仕上げについては、極力手を加えずあえて痕跡として残し、その上に耐震補強という新たな要素を描き重ねることで、新旧の素材の対比が新しい風景を生み出すことを意図した。新たに付加した鉄骨架構が、脆弱な補強CB造に対して、水平方向の剛性を確保すると共に鉛直方向にテンションを加えて、有効な耐震補強として機能する。外部に大きく張り出した新しい架構はパーゴラや雪よけとしても利用可能で、その下には中間領域的な気持ちのいい居場所が生まれた。工事は、RC、鉄骨、大工、屋根、建具の各工事を工務店が担当し、内装、家具、塗装の作業は建築学科学生によるセルフビルドを交えながら施工を行った。

This is a project that involved seismic reinforcement and the conversion of a concrete block apple orchard monitoring outhouse, built by the client's father-in-law, into a common space with multiple functions such as after-school, elder care, and a consumers' co-op station. The existing building skeleton and finishes that had been soaked in the memories of the whole family were intentionally left as "traces" without any modification. New elements, such as seismic reinforcements, were added on top of them to create a new scenery with the contrast between old and new materials. The newly added steel frame structure provides horizontal rigidity and vertical tension to the fragile reinforced concrete block structure, and functions as effective seismic reinforcement. The new structure, which protrudes widely outside, can be used as a support for a pergola or snow shelter, and a comfortable intermediate area was created beneath it. The RC, steel frame, carpentry, roofing, and fittings were constructed by local contractors, while the interior furniture and painting were done by architecture students with the clients in the spirit of self-building.

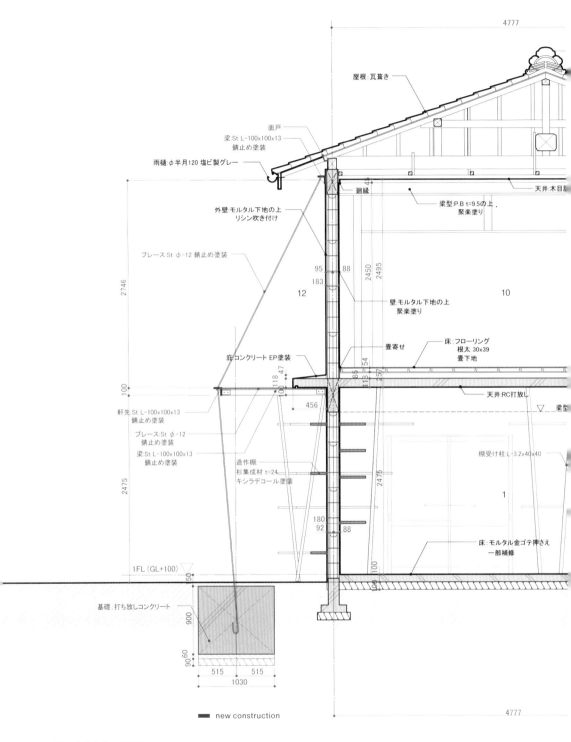

屋根:瓦葺き

面戸

梁:St L-100x100x13
錆止め塗装

雨樋:φ半月120 塩ビ製グレー

廻縁

天井:木目

梁型:P.B t=9.5の上
聚楽塗り

外壁:モルタル下地の上
リシン吹き付け

ブレース:St φ-12 錆止め塗装

壁:モルタル下地の上
聚楽塗り

畳寄せ

床:フローリング
根太 30x39
畳下地

庇コンクリート EP塗装

天井:RC打放し

梁型

軒先:St L-100x100x13
錆止め塗装

ブレース:St φ-12
錆止め塗装

梁:St L-100x100x13
錆止め塗装

棚受け柱 L-3.2x40x40

造作棚
杉集成材 t=24
キシラデコール塗装

1FL (GL+100)

床:モルタル金ゴテ押さえ
一部補修

基礎:打ち放しコンクリート

4777

2746

95   88

183

12

2450

2495

10

100

118
47

456

85
54

4577

2475

2475

1

180
92   88

100

515   515

1030

900

90 60

■ new construction

sectional detail s=1/50

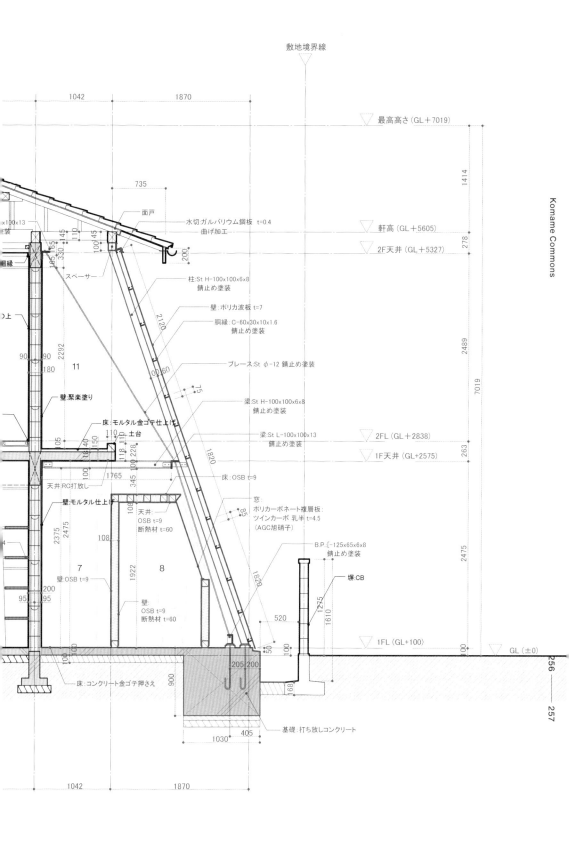

敷地境界線

最高高さ (GL＋7019)

1042　　　1870

735

面戸

水切:ガルバリウム鋼板 t=0.4
曲げ加工

軒高 (GL＋5605)

2F天井 (GL＋5327)

x100x13

隅縁

スペーサー

柱:St H-100x100x6x8
錆止め塗装

壁:ポリカ波板 t=7

胴縁:C-60x30x10x1.6
錆止め塗装

ブレース:St φ-12 錆止め塗装

梁:St H-100x100x6x8
錆止め塗装

壁:聚楽塗り

床:モルタル金ゴテ仕上げ

土台

梁:St L-100x100x13
錆止め塗装

2FL (GL＋2838)

1F天井 (GL＋2575)

床:OSB t=9

天井 RC打放し

壁:モルタル仕上げ

窓:
ポリカーボネート複層板:
ツインカーボ 乳半 t=4.5
(AGC旭硝子)

天井:
OSB t=9
断熱材 t=60

B.P.:[-125x65x6x8
錆止め塗装

7

8

塀:CB

壁:OSB t=9

壁:
OSB t=9
断熱材 t=60

1FL (GL＋100)

GL (±0)

床:コンクリート金ゴテ押さえ

基礎:打ち放しコンクリート

1030　　　405

1042　　　1870

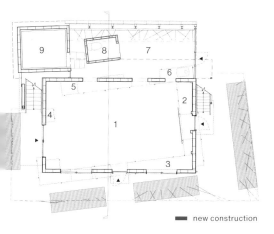

1st floor plan s=1/200

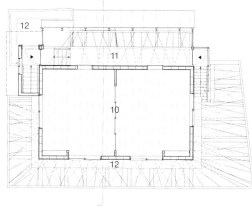

2nd floor plan s=1/200

■ new construction

1 co-op station
2 shelf
3 workbench
4 sorting counter
5 co-op shelf
6 kitchen
7 earthen floor
8 WC
9 den
10 after-school
11 corridor
12 terrace

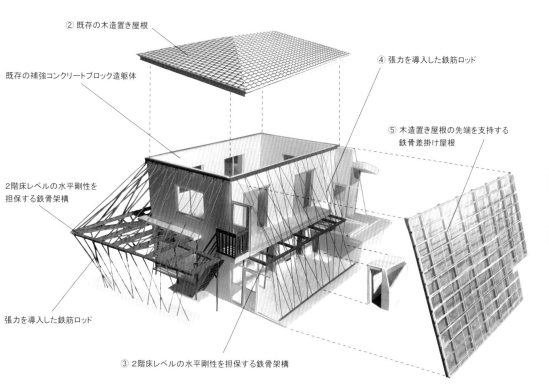

② 既存の木造置き屋根

既存の補強コンクリートブロック造躯体

④ 張力を導入した鉄筋ロッド

⑤ 木造置き屋根の先端を支持する
　鉄骨差掛け屋根

2階床レベルの水平剛性を
担保する鉄骨架構

張力を導入した鉄筋ロッド

③ 2階床レベルの水平剛性を担保する鉄骨架構

キャンパス内の「余地」を
掻き集めて「敷地」を見い出す。

The "site" is found by scraping "surplus space"
on the campus.

大阪市立大学工学部 F棟実験室
Osaka City University Faculty of Engineering
F Building Laboratories

2020

既存校舎に囲まれた2つの中庭に実験室2室と準備室2室を増築する必要があり、工学部F棟のピロティを横断するように、立体的な「余地」を掻き集めて一体の「敷地」を見出している。貴重な中庭の開放感を担保するために、建物は南側に寄せて視線の抜けを確保し、動線を妨げないように4つのヴォリュームに分割して、ピロティには準備室を、ダクト配管のため天井高が必要な実験室はピロティ部を外して、全体としては雁行するような配置としている。外装材としては、雑多な仕上げを持つ古い校舎群にも馴染むように、あえて全く異なる風合いを持つコールテン鋼板を選択した。特に屋根面については校舎群からの見下ろしに配慮して第5のファサードと位置付け、外壁と一体のコールテン鋼板で包み込んでいる。コールテン鋼板表面の表情については、仮置きで生じた雨掛かりや水溜りの跡を気にせず、信楽焼きのように偶然に現れたあるがままの表情を楽しむこととした。

Given a limited site, we had to add two laboratories and preparation rooms each, so we gathered a three-dimensional "space" crossing the 'pilotis' of the existing building and discovered a site. Within the limited site, we placed the additions on the south side to ensure that the openness of the courtyard was not lost and also to secure the line of sight. It was divided into four volumes to secure the necessary outdoor circulation flow. The preparation rooms were arranged within the 'pilotis' with a low ceiling height, while the laboratories that require sufficient ceiling height for ducting were placed outside. The overall arrangement is like that of a goose-flying formation. For the exterior material, we chose COR-TEN steel plate, a contrasting texture that fits in with the myriad of old buildings' materials. Considering that people can overlook down on the additions from the existing buildings, the roof surface was positioned as the fifth façade, and finished in COR-TEN steel plate to create an integrated surface with the walls.

G棟

F棟

R棟

10 10 8 10 9 1 2 5 4 3 7 6 10 10

■ new addition   ▨ existing   1st floor plan s=1/500

Osaka City University Faculty of Engineering F Building Laboratories

1 biotechnology laboratory
2 biotechnology preparation room
3 applied chemistry laboratory
4 applied chemistry preparation room
5 pilotis
6 pump room
7 water tank
8 electrical room
9 mound
10 planting
11 corridor
12 laboratory

12	11	12
12	11	12
12	11	12
12	11	12

| 1 | 2 | 5 | 4 | 3 |

Exp.J   Exp.J

A-A' section s=1/500

Roof
COR-TEN steel t:6
Sprayed cement base rockwool t:75

1.400
900 500 270

Fiber Cement board t:6
Rockwool insulation t:90

Recessed pelmet
Synthetic resin paint finish

Metal coverplate t:2.3 bent to shape
Anti condensation foam backing t:4
Waterproofing sheet

Metal cover plate t:1.6

Ceiling
Gypsum board t:12.5+9.5 in emulsion paint finish
Light gauge steel framing

Ceiling
Gypsum board t:12.5+9.5 in emulsion paint finish
Light gauge steel framing

Existing F-Building Ceiling
Aluminium spandrel panel
Light gauge steel framing

COR-TEN steel plate t:3.2
Fluorine-based matte clear paint finish

Aluminum spandrel panel

Wall
Gypsum board t:12.5+9.5
in emulsion paint finish

Wall
Gypsum board t:12.5+9.5
in emulsion paint finish

Wall
COR-TEN steel plate t:3.2
Rockwool insulation t:90

1   2   5

Floor
Vinyl flooring sheet
Water resistant plywood t:12
Particle board t:20
Metal raised floor supports

Floor
Vinyl flooring sheet
Screed to level t:100-130 with welded steel mesh reinforcement
over existing floor

D10 Steel reinforcement bars
@600 L:900

Screed to level t:100-130 with
welded steel mesh reinforcement Φ-6·100x100

Polystyrene foam t:30
Damp proof sheet
Gravel

Exp.J

3.900   3.900   2.230   720   4.370   2.730

B-B' sectional detail s=1/125

太鼓橋をくぐり抜け、
風車の中で遊ぶ。

Passing under the arched bridge,
and playing in the "windmill."

上郡町立認定こども園

Kamigori Nursery School

2021

4棟の園舎を風車型に配置することにより、セキュリティの高い中庭型でありながら閉鎖的になり過ぎない保育・教育環境をつくることを目指した。外部からは園舎と園舎の隙間を通してこどもたちの活動が垣間見え、園内からは屋根越しに周辺の山並みを望むことができる。またエントランス部に太鼓橋を掛けることによって上履きと下履きの動線を立体交差させ、中庭側から直接登園できるようにした。中庭の周りには縁側が巡り、そこに大きく庇が張り出している。4棟の妻側にも切妻屋根が伸びて、大きな半屋外空間をつくる。純粋な室内空間の面積が927m²であるのに対して、開放可能な回廊空間と軒下空間を合わせると半屋外空間は874m²にもなる。インテリアについては、自然なかたちで場所に対するアイデンティティが育まれるように、最長6年に及ぶこどもの発達段階に応じて少しずつスケールや仕上げ、色といった空間の質と風景が変化するように細やかなデザインを心がけた。

By arranging four wooden buildings with different functions around a courtyard in a windmill shape, we wanted to create an open and highly secure education and childcare space. From the outside, one can catch a glimpse of children's activities through the gap between the buildings, and from within the garden, the children and teachers have a view of the surrounding mountains over the roof. The three-dimensional intersection of exterior and interior shoe-use circulation lines facilitated by the arched bridge allows one to enter directly into the buildings from the courtyard. Another feature is that there is a large semi-outdoor space. The deep eaves over the veranda go around the courtyard, and the gable ends are also extended to create a large sheltered space. The area of absolute indoor space is 927 m², while the open sheltered spaces comes up to a total of 874 m². We designed the interior so that the scale, finish, and color change little by little according to the growth of the child for up to 6 years in order to create an environment where children can easily form an identity naturally with the place naturally.

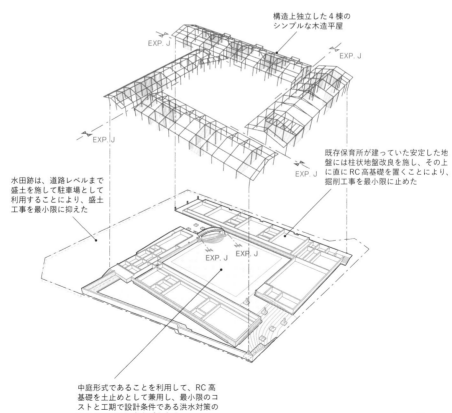

構造上独立した4棟の
シンプルな木造平屋

EXP. J

EXP. J

EXP. J

既存保育所が建っていた安定した地
盤には柱状地盤改良を施し、その上
に直にRC高基礎を置くことにより、
掘削工事を最小限に止めた

EXP. J

水田跡は、道路レベルまで
盛土を施して駐車場として
利用することにより、盛土
工事を最小限に抑えた

EXP. J   EXP. J

EXP. J

中庭形式であることを利用して、RC高
基礎を土止めとして兼用し、最小限のコ
ストと工期で設計条件である洪水対策の
ための1m弱の嵩上げを実現

structure diagram

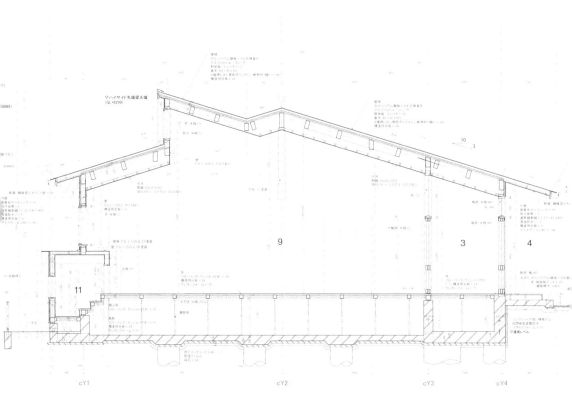

sectional detail s=1/100

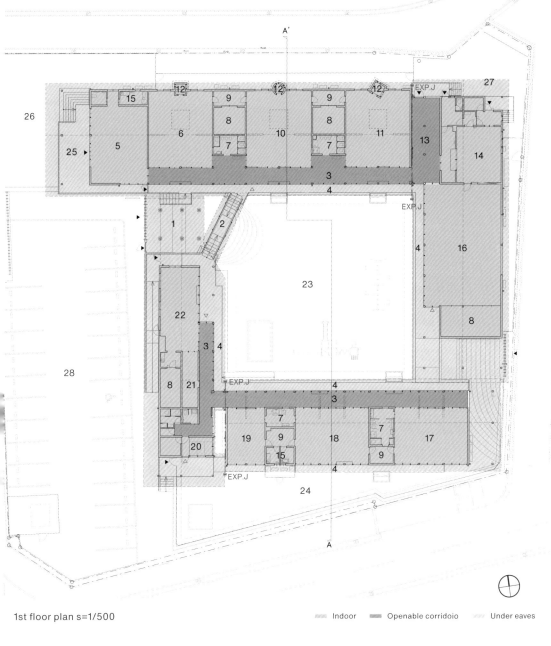

1st floor plan s=1/500

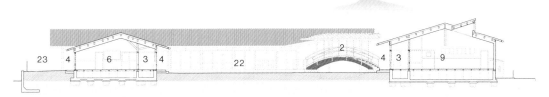

A-A' section s=1/400

1 porch	8 nursery room (3 years old)	15 library	22 courtyard
2 arched bridge	9 nursery room (4 years old)	16 teachers' room	23 garden
3 corridor	10 nursery room (5 years old)	17 infirmary	24 kitchen service loading and parking
4 veranda	11 den	18 break room	25 parking
5 infant room	12 childcare support room	19 WC	
6 toddler room	13 playroom	20 bath and nursing room	
7 nursery room (2 years old)	14 kitchen	21 storage	

「三方格子」と鉄板で
組み上げた、屋根の量塊。

A massive roof assembled
with the "triaxial wooden lattice" and steel plates.

常泉寺新位牌堂
Josen-ji Temple Tablet Hall

2022

1000基の位牌を祀る位牌堂である。延焼と裏山の土砂崩れに備えて本堂との接続部はRC造とし、木造の軒同士が迫り合う部分についても空中に防火壁を浮かべて延焼を防いでいる。屋根のフォルムは、裏山の墓地からの見下ろしに配慮して、ヴォリューム感のある七寸勾配の寄棟とした。西側玄関の前は大きく吹き放ちとして土庇を設け、管理用の車動線を確保している。広間は葬儀も可能な無柱空間とするために、小屋組に陶器浩一考案の三方格子と呼ぶ立体格子を用いた。最初に耐力壁となる4枚のRCキャンティ壁を立て、その上に三方格子と鉄板で構成したハイブリッドの小屋組を載せている。広間の外周には縁が巡る。縁先に立つ木造列柱は、広間四隅と土庇の丸柱と共に軸力を負担する。柱と小屋組の接合部は構造的に多くの材を積み重ねる必要があったことから、あえて斗栱を意識した組物とした。内陣には防火上の理由から陣笠のような鉄板の天蓋を掛け、床も瓦敷きとしている。

This is a Buddhist mortuary tablet hall where 1,000 tablets are enshrined. In order to prevent the spread of fire and landslides from the hill behind the building, the connection with the main temple hall is made of RC, and a fire wall is floated in the air to prevent the spread of fire where the wooden eaves meet each other. The roof form is a voluminous 7/10-sloped hipped roof, in consideration of the view from the cemetery at the back of the building. In front of the west side entrance, a large open earthen floor is provided to secure the passage for maintenance vehicles. In order to make the hall a pillar-less space where a funeral can be held, a three-dimensional lattice called "Mikata Lattice," developed by Kazuhiro Toki, is used for the framework. Four RC cantilever walls were first erected as load-bearing walls, and then a hybrid structure consisting of "Mikata Lattice" and steel plates was placed on top. The perimeter of the hall is surrounded by a veranda. The wooden columns standing at the edge of the veranda bear the vertical forces, together with the round columns at the four corners of the hall and the ones at the earthen floor eaves. The joints between the columns and the roof frame lattice were designed to resemble a *to-kyo* (a traditional wooden bracket structure), as it was structurally necessary to stack up many pieces of timber. The altar floor is finished with clay tiles and is also covered with a steel canopy for fire protection.

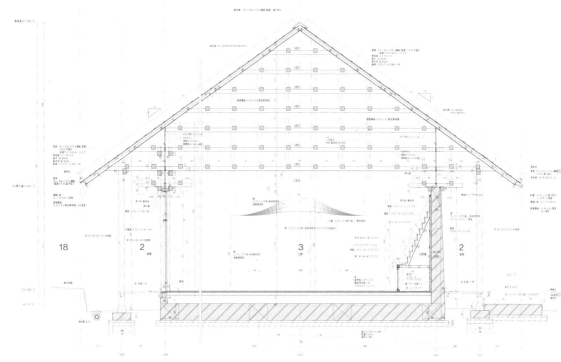

A-A' sectional detail s=1/100

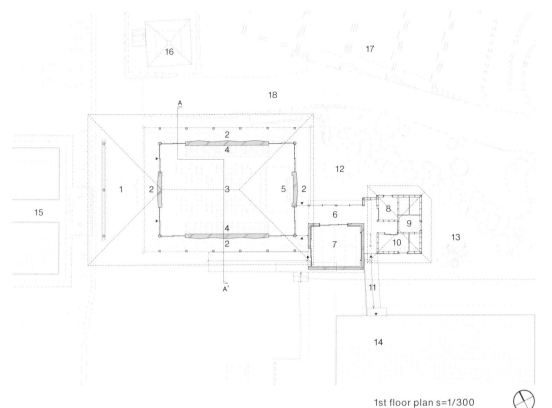

1st floor plan s=1/300

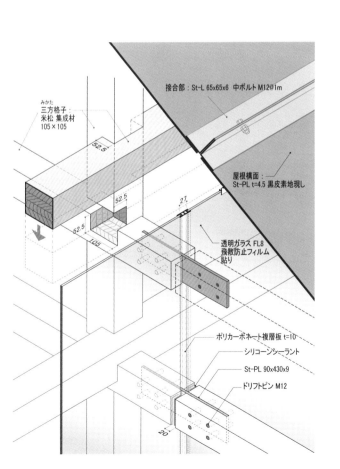

接合部：St-L 65x65x6 中ボルト M12@1m

みかた
三方格子：
米松 集成材
105×105

52.5
52.5
52.5
105
27
20

屋根構面：
St-PL t=4.5 黒皮素地現し

透明ガラス FL8
飛散防止フィルム
貼り

ポリカーボネート複層板 t=10

シリコーンシーラント

St-PL 90x430x9

ドリフトピン M12

1 porch
2 veranda
3 hall
4 tablet altar
5 altar
6 corridor
7 multipurpose room
8 storage
9 WC (f)
10 WC (m)
11 bridge
12 garden 1
13 garden 2
14 main hall
15 storehouse
16 shrine
17 cemetery
18 ramp

exisitng

「文化財」的建築を背景に、埋蔵「文化財」を鑑賞する。

Appreciating the buried "cultural properties" against the background of the "cultural property" architecture.

北九州市立埋蔵文化財センター（旧八幡市民会館のコンヴァージョン）

Kitakyushu Archaeological Center (Conversion and Rejuvenation of the former Yahata Civic Hall)

estimated in 2025

村野藤吾設計の八幡市民会館（1958年竣工）を埋蔵文化財センターへとコンバージョンするプロジェクトである。オリジナルデザインを極力保全しながらも、新しい用途に対応するために新たなデザインを大胆に付加している。新たなデザインは必ずしも村野調の模倣ではなく、むしろ新旧デザインが調和して、全体として新たな建築的価値を持つように努めた。最大の空間ヴォリュームが必要となる収蔵庫は旧ホールを転用し、ステージを客席側へ延長して広くフラットな床を確保する。観客は区画されたガラスボックスのなかから、村野オリジナルの特徴的なラッカー仕上げラワンベニアの壁を背景に、あえて奥行き感が出るようにレイアウトした収蔵棚が整然と並ぶ「見える収蔵庫」を鑑賞することになる。他にも展示計画やディテールを含めてさまざまな工夫を積み重ねて、建築という「文化財」を背景にして埋蔵「文化財」を鑑賞するという貴重な体験を多様な側面から楽しめる計画としている。

This is a project to convert 'Yahata Civic Hall' (completed in 1958) designed by Togo Murano into an archaeological center. While preserving Murano's original design as much as possible, a new design is boldly added to accommodate the new use. The new design is not necessarily an imitation of the Murano style but rather a harmonization of the old and new designs, so that the building as a whole has new architectural value. The storage room, which requires the largest spatial volume, is converted from the old main hall, and the stage is extended to the audience side to secure a wide, flat floor. From the compartmentalized glass box, visitors can see the "visible storage," where storage shelves are arranged orderly to create a sense of depth with a background of Murano's original peculiar lacquered Lauan veneer walls. The exhibition plan and architectural details are also designed to allow visitors to enjoy the precious experience of viewing buried "cultural properties" against the backdrop of architectural "cultural property" from a variety of perspectives.

「料」と「理」の*menu*

八幡市民会館から北九州市立埋蔵文化財センターへの転用改修における素材と調理法

Materials and Cooking Methods in the Conversion and Rejuvenation of
the former Yahata Civil Hall to the Kitakyushu Archaeological Center

1

埋蔵文化財の
文化財建築包み

*Les biens culturels exhumés,
emballés de patrimoine architectural*

埋蔵文化財センターは地域毎に設けられ、埋蔵文化財の発掘調査・研究・収蔵・展示等を行う公共機関であるが、実際のところ一般市民にとってあまり馴染みがあるとは言い難い。北九州市立埋蔵文化財センターでは、来館者が「文化財」級の建築物を背景にして埋蔵「文化財」を鑑賞するという稀有な体験を楽しむことで、文化財同士が相乗効果を生むことが期待される。

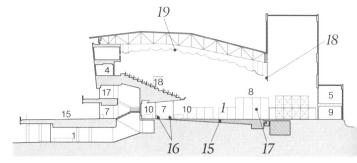

section s=1/800

⊕

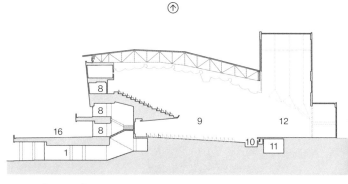

section（exisitng）s=1/800

1	entrance hall	10	orchestra pit
2	office	11	trap cellar
3	exhibition room	12	stage
4	workshop	13	greenroom
5	storage	14	meeting room
6	mechanical	15	art gallery
7	areaway	16	driveway apron
8	foyer	17	chimney
9	seating	18	spotlight booth

▬▬ demolition

1	entrance hall	10	"visible storage"
2	office	11	workshop
3	training room	12	studio
4	storage	13	chimney
5	mechanical	14	service entry
6	areaway	15	terrace
7	exhibition room	16	outdoor exhibition
8	collection storage	17	exhibition (Yahata civic hall memorial)
9	special collection storage	18	observation box

▬▬ new volume

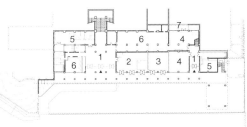

basement floor plan (exisitng) s=1/1500

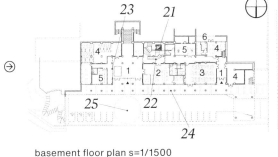

basement floor plan s=1/1500

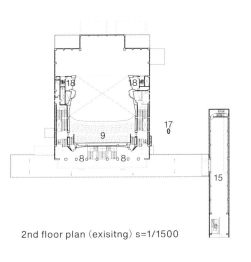

1st floor plan (exisitng) s=1/1500

1st floor plan s=1/1500

2nd floor plan (exisitng) s=1/1500

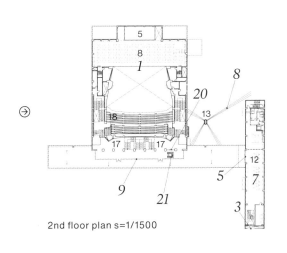

2nd floor plan s=1/1500

2 コールテン鋼板を エキスパンド加工した軽やかなグリル

Un léger grillé d'acier Corten en métal déployé

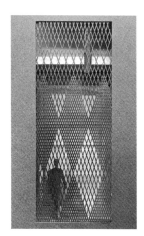

旧村野・森
建築事務所の
門扉

コールテン鋼板を加工した番手の大きなエキスパンドメタルを適宜切断して、大小の菱型文様を生かしたグリルをつくる。手法自体は村野藤吾が編み出したものである。

⊕

3 "奥二重のビューティー" 鉄骨耐震補強の下地窓風

"La beauté du double tranchant discret"
——La construction parasismique en acier
rappelant l'esthétique du "Shitaji-mado"
(fenêtre japonais installée dans une partie
non plâtrée d'un mur de boue)

村野藤吾自邸の
下地窓風開口部

旧美術展示棟に必要となるマンサード型の鉄骨耐震補強をあえて見せて、下地窓風に仕上げた開口部。コールテン鋼板の開口の奥にさらにアスロックパネル開口を重ねて、深みのあるファサードをつくる。ガラスは最大製作寸法を越えるため、ステンレス製カバーの付いた方立を1本立てて分割している。阪神淡路大震災で失われてしまった村野藤吾自邸の居間と中廊下の間に設けられた下地窓風開口部の本歌取りでもある。

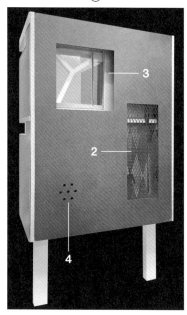

旧美術展示棟妻面のために新たにデザインした
コールテン鋼板のファサード

4 七つ星の穴あき

Le panneau perforé au motif
de constellation 7 étoiles

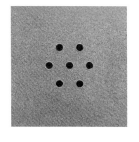

コールテン鋼板に開けた7つの穴。彫刻家福岡道雄の晩年に『つぶ3つ』や『つぶ7つ』と題した作品があるが、そんな諧謔と諦念を通り越した自由な境地に早くたどり着きたいものだ。

5 大ぶりなガラスにガラスブロックをあしらった外付けウィンドウ

Les fenêtres extérieures constituées
de vastes panneaux de verre avec de briques de verre

整理作業室は元々窓の少ない旧展示室からの転用であるため、居室としての快適性を求めて1、2階に一つずつ大きな開口部を設ける。透明ガラスとガラスブロックで構成した開口部のサッシュは溶融亜鉛ドブ漬けメッキとし、躯体に開けた穴よりも大きく覆うように外壁面に外付けとして、後補であることをあえて明示している。

Kitakyushu Archaeological Center

6 浅く曲げたコールテン鋼板の親子唐破風 ——両班の笠帽子갓から下がる갓끈風の竪樋を添えて

Le "Karahafu" en croupe et demi-croupe en acier Corten légèrement courbée
——Les avant-toits évoquant le "Gat" (chapeau de dignitaire coréen, 갓),
accompagnés d'une gouttière en forme de "Gakkun" (cordon de chapeau, 갓끈)

旧美術展示棟から1階テラスへの出入り口と、同じく新たに設けた埋蔵文化財の洗い場に雨除けが必要になり、コールテン鋼板を曲げて唐破風風の庇をデザインすることとした。縦樋のデザインが難しいところだが、外壁面に沿って素直に垂直に立てることを選んだ。どこかで見たことがある形だと思ったら、韓流ドラマ時代劇で見かけるアレ、貴族が被る帽子갓(カッ)であった。下がり紐の部分は갓끈(カックン)と言うそうである。

7 1958年産RCのスペアリブを削ぎ落しで

Les côtes levées de RC 1958, totalement dénudées

幸いなことに工事写真が市によって丁寧に保管されていた。そこには70年近く前のコンクリート型枠工事の風景が写っていた(左上)。バラ板型枠を使った手の跡が残る素朴なコンクリートである。旧美術展示棟は、屋根は防水の改修に合わせて外断熱に変更することから、1・2階共に天井を撤去して規則正しく並ぶ柱梁のスケルトンを打放しのまま見せることとした。

8 "だれが見ても分かる煙突の耐震補強"
皿倉山のシルエットに重なる12本の白のロッド添え

Le renforcement sismique de la cheminée servit avec 12 tiges blanches très présentes, soulignant la silhouette du mont Sarakura

この格好の良い煙突が具体的にどういう幾何学的形状をしているのかを把握したのは、村野・森建築事務所の担当者以外ではおそらく私たち設計チームだけではないだろうか。それくらい複雑な形状をしている。しかし、いくら調べても基礎については図面も情報も見つからない。したがって、しっかりとした基礎が存在しないという前提で耐震補強を計画せざるを得なかった。中間部くびれの少し上部からPC鋼より線12本で四方に引っ張って、足元の自動車動線を避けながら地面にアンカーすることとした。それが背後に聳える皿倉山の稜線の角度に一致したのは偶然である。

9 レンガタイルをまとった量塊（ヴォリューム）を
軽やかに支える形鋼でつくったサッシュ

Les cadres de fenêtre en acier portant avec légèreté la masse recouverte de carreaux brique

建築史家の笠原一人（京都工芸繊維大学）は、旧八幡市民会館の最大の特徴は重たげなレンガの量塊がガラスの水平スリットの上部に浮いていることだと言う。その矛盾した表現こそが村野藤吾の魅力だと。しかしながら、実のところ当時の技術ではスチールサッシュは必ずしも軽やかにはつくれなかったのではないか。未完のコンセプトをそのまま受け継ぎ、いまいち重たげな老朽化したサッシュをより軽快なデザインの形鋼を使ったスチールサッシュに取り替える。

←

10 中庭にそよぐ竹林のスクリーン
──細長いミドルヤードを透して

L'écran à la vue des bambous dansant au gré du vent ──un regard porté à travers le long couloir étroit

旧ホール棟と旧美術展示棟を繋ぐミドルヤードのヴォリュームは極めて細長い。幅は4m弱しかなく、しかも両面共ほぼ全面ガラス張りである。したがって正面から見ると建築を透して背後の中庭がよく見通せる。そこに村野好みの孟宗竹を植えることとした。（右写真は箱根プリンスホテル中庭の孟宗林）

→

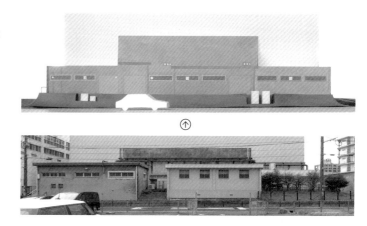

11

既存開口部と新設ベントキャップが奏でる"アリエッタ"

L'"ariette" des fenêtres d'antan et des coiffes d'aération d'aujourd'hui

老朽化した空調・換気設備はほぼ総入れ替えする予定である。それにともなって外壁に現れるさまざまな吸排気口、換気口は、既存開口部とのバランスも見ながらある秩序を持ってレイアウトするように努めた。楽譜のように見えなくもない。

12

剥き出しになった開口部の楽しげなリズムのモルタル縁取りレンガタイル詰め ── 撤去された増築部の微かな痕跡を彩りに添えて

Le joyeux rythme des carreaux brique d'encadrement en mortier sur les ouvertures dénudées, accompagné des subtiles traces de l'extension démolie

旧ホール棟のフライタワー背後（南側）には元々楽屋等のヴォリュームが下屋状に設けられていたが、機能的な必要性に迫られてさまざまな雑多なヴォリュームが増築されて、最後は見るも無残な姿になっていた。増築ヴォリューム自体は解体撤去することに決まったものの、それでも既存部にどうしても痕跡は残る。また工事用の搬出入ルートも南面に設けられると想定される。埋められていた開口部には改めてレンガタイルを貼る等、さまざまな痕跡を丁寧にトレースするように新しいデザインを組み立て直したい。

13

バックステージ裏から彫り出したRC打放ちの"エプロン"

Le "tablier" en béton brut déterré des coulisses

旧ホール棟南側増築部の撤去にともなって、既存部下屋の基礎が剥き出しになることが判明した。そこで前面道路と下屋を馴染ませるようにアールの付いた袴状のエプロンを設けることとした。結果的に基壇が「彫り出された」ということになる。

14 解体現場から"発掘"された 鉱滓レンガを積んだ屋外展示台

Le plateau d'exposition hors-mur en brique de laitier "excavés" de sites de démolition

鉱滓レンガ

既存建物の内壁仕上げの背後には、間仕切り壁等として鉱滓レンガが積まれていることが調査で明らかになっている。村野も好んだ鉱滓レンガは、製鉄の副産物として排出される鉱滓を混入して焼成したレンガである。不要となった鉱滓レンガを丁寧に解体して取り分け、改めて積み直して屋外の展示台として再利用する。

15 "埋没文化財" —— 延長されたステージに沈む観客席

Le bien culturel submergé —— les fauteuils immergés sous la nouvelle scène prolongée

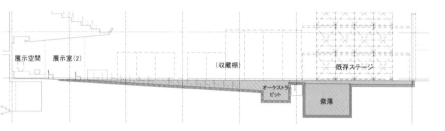

展示空間　展示室(2)　(収蔵棚)　既存ステージ　オーケストラピット　奈落

多数の収蔵棚を設置するために、既存ステージを客席側へ延長してフラットで丈夫な床を確保する必要があった。結果的に（あくまでイメージ上の話として、、）スロープ上に配された既存客席は水平な新設床に徐々に沈んで行き、そこに"埋没"する"文化財"を感じてしまった。

16 延長されたステージのスープに浸んでゆく 客席を利用したガラス衝突防止のための手摺

Les fauteuils réappropriés à la balustrade protectrice immergeant dans la "soupe" d'estrade élargie

展示室内では既存の客席が（イメージの上だけではなく、、実際に足元が延長されたステージに少し沈む形で保存される。それは観賞者用の椅子であり、同時に大きなガラス面への衝突防止のための手摺としても機能する。

→

17 "テアトロ・オリンピコ"
バックライトに浮かび上がる
逆パースのついた収蔵棚

*Le "Teatro Olimpico" —— les étagères de
conservation nichées dans une perspective inversée
illuminées par un contre-jour*

旧ホールの南側、バックステージの東西両サイドには、自然採光のための大きなハイサイドライトが設けられる。南北方向に整然と配置した収蔵棚は奥側（南側）ほど背が高く、ハイサイドライトからの逆光によって荘厳に浮かび上がる。アンドレア・パラディオ他による遠近法を強調した立体書き割り"テアトロ・オリンピコ"を連想してしまった。

18 "森村泰昌からの贈りもの"
京都産のカーテン生地を再利用した
プロセニアムのドレープ飾り

*"Un cadeau de l'artiste Yasumasa Morimura"
—— La tenture de proscenium faite des rideaux
de Kyoto recyclés*

展覧会で使用した資材をそのまま廃棄するのはいかにももったいない。「アート・シマツ」と呼ぶプロジェクトは、そんな思いを持った美術家の森村泰昌さんの呼び掛けで始まった。京都市京セラ美術館で開催された『森村泰昌：ワタシの迷宮劇場』（2022年）で使われたカーテン生地を譲り受けて、プロセニアムのドレープ飾りのように使うことで、ここがかつて劇場であった記憶を伝えてゆきたい。

19 優美な天井を剥くと現れる豪快な屋根トラス
——"エンガワ"は残して

*Sur le plafond gracieux démantelé de manière à préserver l'"Engawa",
se révèle la charpente de toit audacieuse*

優美な曲線を描く既存天井は建築基準法上の特定天井に該当し、脱落・落下を防止する対策が必要であった。しかし下地は木製の上、老朽化も著しく、現実問題としては解体撤去せざるを得なかった。一方で天井解体の結果剥き出しとなる屋根の鉄骨トラスは、映画のロケで使われたこともある迫力のある架構であり、収蔵庫の天井としてはむしろそれを積極的にデザインとして活用することとした。さらに特定天井に該当せずに済む200m²のみを軽い材料で"エンガワ"状に復元する。

20

籐で編んだ"おにぎり"型のランプシェードをあしらった 無骨な鉄骨耐震補強ブレース

L'Abat-jour en forme d'"Onigiri", délicatement tissés en rotin, diffusant une lumière douce et tamisée sur le renfort sismique en acier brut

ホワイエの真ん中に無骨な耐震補強を施すことが必要であった。そこでV字型の鉄骨ブレースを、籐で編んだ半透明のシェードを"おにぎり"の形にして優しく包み込み、全体を大きな照明器具のように見せることとした。

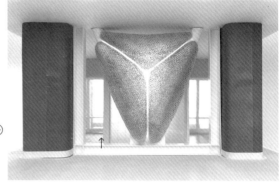

21

"光の井戸"として機能する ガラスブロックのEVシャフト

Le "puits de lumière" d'ascenseur en brique de verre, éclairant le souterrain

バリアフリー改修のためのエレベーター設置場所の選定については苦労した。各階の平面が全てズレているからである。結果的に地下1階の旧機械室をエレベーターホールに転用することで、何とか一般開放エリア同士を垂直に繋ぐことが出来た。さらにエレベーターシャフトをガラスブロックでつくることにより、窓のない旧機械室に光を導いている。

22

つづらに折れたスロープと階段で つくった段差解消のためのマウンド

La colline en zig-zag, associant des escaliers et des rampes pour éliminer les dénivelés

エレベーターを地下1階まで下ろせはしたものの、実はさらにその下にあるフーチングにぶつかって旧機械室の床レベルに着床することが出来なかった。幸いエレベーターホールとしては充分過ぎる広さを持っていたので、スロープと階段から成る楽しげなマウンドを築いて90cmの段差を解消している。

23　城野遺跡石棺展示のために撤去した既存壁のニュアンスをあえて残したエントランスホール

Le mur d'entrée démantelé à contrecœur,
laissant entrevoir les cicatrices de son retrait aux côtés
des sarcophages antiques de Jyono

メインエントランスホールには収蔵品として最も価値のある大型の城野遺跡石棺を展示することに決まったが、充分な鑑賞スペースを取ることが出来なかった。そこで既存壁を撤去して、隣接する旧チケット売り場までエントランスホールを拡張することとしたが、壁の撤去跡はあえて残して市民会館時代の記憶を伝えるように配慮している。

Kitakyushu Archaeological Center

24　二丁掛けタイル矢矧ぎ貼りのコロネードに導かれるアプローチ

La colonnade décorée de tuiles allongées
dans un motif de chevron, guidant élégamment
les pas des passagers vers l'entrée

旧市民会館正面の土地を隣接する市立八幡病院の駐車場として譲ったため、埋蔵文化財センターとしての正規のアプローチは自ずと西側の前面道路から続くコロネード（列柱廊）経由となる。長いコロネードを歩いた上で突然右に直角に折れて正面玄関へ至る。いかにも不自然な動線を少しでも右斜め方向へと意識づける床のデザインとして二丁掛けタイル矢矧ぎ貼りを選んでいる。それは村野藤吾自邸玄関土間で用いられたデザインの大仰な「写し」である。

村野藤吾自邸玄関土間

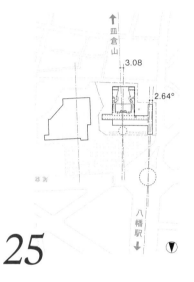

25

"メダイヨン"　ピンコロ石で仕上げた円形のハンプ ──皿倉山への軸線と平行する病院グリッドを補正する気持ちを込めて

Le "médaillon"──Une bosse en pinkorie
pour ajuster la grille de stationnement
de l'hôpital avec l'axe menant au mont Sarakura

旧美術展示棟は八幡駅から伸びる平和通りと同じ角度で配置されたように見えるが、実際には2.64度振れている。復興平和記念像の立つラウンドアバウトがこの微妙な角度を補正している。隣接する市立八幡病院とその駐車場の軸はたまたま八幡のシンボル皿倉山山頂を向くが、旧八幡市民会館とは3.08度振れている。正面玄関前に円形のハンプを設けることにより、ラウンドアバウトと同じくこの角度を補正すると共に、歩行者の安全を図る計画である。

Data

46

Open-Air Kindergarten

所在地：兵庫県宝塚市
用途：幼稚園
竣工：1992年
延床面積：72 m²
構造／規模：S造、RC造／地下1階、地上1階
構造設計者：今川憲英（TIS）

Location: Takarazuka City, Hyogo Pref.
Principal use: kindergarten
Completion year: 1992
Total floor area: 72 m²
Structure: steel frame, reinforced
concrete／1 basement and 1 story
Structural engineer:
Norihide Imagawa (TIS)

───────────

52

家族文化アパートメント「愛田荘」
AIDA-SOU: Apartment House for Family

所在地：兵庫県宝塚市
用途：集合住宅
竣工：1995年
延床面積：198 m²
構造／規模：木造、一部RC造／地上2階

Location: Takarazuka City, Hyogo Pref.
Principal use: apartment house
Completion year: 1995
Total floor area: 198 m²
Structure: wood, partly reinforced
concrete／2 stories

───────────

62

「ゼンカイ」ハウス
House Surgery ("ZENKAI" HOUSE)

所在地：兵庫県宝塚市
用途：アトリエ
竣工：1997年
延床面積：89 m²
構造／規模：木造、S造／地上2階
構造設計者：
外村静夫（アスコラル構造研究所）

Location: Takarazuka City, Hyogo Pref.
Principal use: architectural studio
Completion year: 1997
Total floor area: 89 m²
Structure: wood structure reinforced
with steel frame／2 stories
Structural engineer:
Shizuo Tonomura (ASCORAL)

───────────

80

南芦屋浜団地コミュニティ＆アート計画
"Sacrificatio"
Sacrificatio: Community & Art Project
for Minami-Ashiyahama Public Housing
Complex

所在地：兵庫県芦屋市
竣工：1998年
用途：モニュメント
敷地面積：約42,000 m²
施工面積：4,234 m²
構造／規模：コンクリート造／全長約400m
構造設計者：今川憲英（TIS）

Location: Ashiya City, Hyogo Pref.
Principal use: monument
Completion year: 1998
Site area: approx.42,000 m²
Built area: 4,234 m²
Structure: concrete／approx.400m length
Structural engineer:
Norihide Imagawa (TIS)

───────────

88

SH@64

所在地：兵庫県西宮市
用途：専用住宅
竣工：1999年
延床面積：136 m²
構造／規模：木造、一部RC造／地上2階
構造設計者：
田口雅一（Tac-D建築構造事務所）

Location: Nishinomiya City, Hyogo Pref.
Principal use: residence
Completion year: 1999
Total floor area: 136 m²
Structure: wood and partly reinforced
concrete／2 stories
Structural engineer:
Masaichi Taguchi (Tac-D)

───────────

96

ヒ

所在地：兵庫県神戸市須磨区
用途：専用住宅
竣工：2000年
延床面積：164 m²
構造／規模：RC造、木造／地上2階+ロフト
構造設計者：池田昌弘建築研究所

Location: Suma-ku, Kobe City, Hyogo Pref.
Principal use: residence
Completion year: 2000
Total floor area: 164 m²
Structure: reinforced concrete, wood／
2 stories and loft
Structural engineer:
Masahiro Ikeda Architecture Studio

───────────

102

苦楽園
KURAKUEN

所在地：兵庫県西宮市
用途：専用住宅
竣工：2001年
延床面積：187 m²

構造／規模：S造、RC造、一部SRC造／
地下1階、地上2階+ロフト
構造設計者：
田口雅一（Tac-D建築構造事務所）

Location: Nishinomiya City, Hyogo Pref.
Principal use: residence
Completion year: 2001
Total floor area: 187 m²
Structure: steel frame, reinforced
concrete, partly steel-reinforced
concrete／1 basement, 2 stories and loft
Structural engineer:
Masaichi Taguchi (Tac-D)

───────────

114

苦楽園の増築
KURAKUEN Addition

竣工：2003年
延床面積：22 m²
構造／規模：膜構造／地上1階
構造設計者：
田口雅一（TAPS建築構造計画事務所）

Completion year: 2003年
Total floor area: 22 m²
Structure: membrane structures／1 story
Structural engineer:
Masaichi Taguchi (TAPS)

───────────

115

苦楽園の離れ
KURAKUEN Annex

竣工：2008年
延床面積：12 m²
構造／規模：木造／地上1階
構造設計者：
田口雅一（TAPS建築構造計画事務所）

Completion year: 2008
Total floor area: 12 m²
Structure: wood／1 story
Structural engineer:
Masaichi Taguchi (TAPS)

───────────

116

スガルカラハフ
SUGARUKARAHAFU

所在地：大阪府大東市
用途：寺院庫裏
竣工：2002年
延床面積：559 m²（増築部分43 m²）
構造／規模：S造、RC造、木造／
地上1階+ロフト
構造設計者：
田口雅一（TAPS建築構造計画事務所）

Location: Daito City, Osaka Pref.
Principal use: temple priests' quarters
Completion year: 2002
Total floor area: 559 m²

(additional area: 43 m²)
Structure: steel frame, reinforced
concrete, wood／1 story and loft
Structural engineer:
Masaichi Taguchi (TAPS)

———————

124

S。H。

所在地：兵庫県宝塚市
用途：SOHO付住宅
竣工：2003年
延床面積：104 m²
構造／規模：S造、一部RC造 ／地上3階
構造設計者：
田口雅一（TAPS建築構造計画事務所）

Location: Takarazuka City, Hyogo Pref.
Principal use: residence with a
workspace
Completion year: 2003
Total floor area: 104 m²
Structure: steel frame, partly reinforced
concrete／3 stories
Structural engineer:
Masaichi Taguchi (TAPS)

———————

130

湊町アンダーグラウンドプロジェクト
Minatomachi Underground Project

開催地：なにわトンネル
（大阪府大阪市浪速区）
用途：インスタレーション
開催年：2003年
共同出品作家：久保田テツ、
"seesaw"（雨森信＋甲斐賢治）、高橋匡太

Location: Naniwa tunnel (Naniwa-ku,
Osaka City, Osaka Pref.)
Principal use: installation
Exhibition Date: 2003
Co-exhibitor: Tetsu Kubota,
"seesaw" (Nov Amenomori + Kenji Kai),
Kyota Takahashi

———————

134

SHIP

所在地：兵庫県西宮市
用途：専用住宅
竣工：2006年
延床面積：112 m²
構造／規模：鉄板造、RC造／
地下1階、地上2階
構造設計者：
田口雅一（TAPS建築構造計画事務所）

Location: Nishinomiya City, Hyogo Pref.
Principal use: residence
Completion year: 2006
Total floor area: 112 m²
Structure: steel plate, reinforced
concrete／1 basement and 2 stories

———————

Structural engineer:
Masaichi Taguchi (TAPS)

———————

144

grappa

所在地：兵庫県宝塚市
用途：専用住宅
竣工：2006年
延床面積：115 m²
構造／規模：木造、一部RC造／
地下1階、地上2階
構造設計者：
田口雅一（TAPS建築構造計画事務所）

Location: Takarazuka City, Hyogo Pref.
Principal use: residence
Completion year: 2006
Total floor area: 115 m²
Structure: wood, partly reinforced
concrete／1 basement and 2 stories
Structural engineer:
Masaichi Taguchi (TAPS)

———————

152

クローバーハウス
CLOVER HOUSE

所在地：兵庫県西宮市
用途：専用住宅
竣工：2006年
延床面積：76 m²
構造／規模：鉄板造、S造、RC造／
地下1階、地上1階
構造設計者：
田口雅一（TAPS建築構造計画事務所）

Location: Nishinomiya City, Hyogo Pref.
Principal use: residence
Completion year: 2006
Total floor area: 76 m²
Structure: steel plate, steel frame,
reinforced concrete／
1 basement and 1 story
Structural engineer:
Masaichi Taguchi (TAPS)

———————

160

「ハンカイ」ハウス
"HANKAI" HOUSE

所在地：兵庫県明石市
用途：専用住宅
竣工：2007年
延床面積：438 m²（増築部分193 m²）
構造／規模：木造／地上2階
構造設計者：陶器浩一（滋賀県立大学）

Location: Akashi City, Hyogo Pref.
Principal use: residence
Completion year: 2007
Total floor area: 438 m²
(additional area:193 m²)
Structure: wood／2 stories

Structural engineer: Hirokazu Toki
(The University of Shiga Prefecture)

———————

168

between

所在地：兵庫県宝塚市
用途：専用住宅
竣工：2009年
延床面積：129 m²
構造／規模：木造、RC造／地上3階
構造設計者：陶器浩一（滋賀県立大学）、
橋本一郎（エス・キューブ・アソシエイツ）

Location: Takarazuka City, Hyogo Pref.
Principal use: residence
Completion year: 2009
Total floor area: 129 m²
Structure: wood, reinforced concrete／
3 stories
Structural engineers: Hirokazu Toki
(The University of Shiga Prefecture),
Ichiro Hashimoto (S3 Associates Inc.)

———————

174

gather

所在地：大阪府大阪市住吉区
用途：専用住宅
竣工：2009年
延床面積：115 m²（増築部分：4 m²）
構造／規模：木造／地上2階
構造設計者：
田口雅一（TAPS建築構造計画事務所）

Location: Sumiyoshi-ku, Osaka City,
Osaka Pref.
Principal use: residence
Completion year: 2009
Total floor area: 115 m²
(additional area: 4 m²)
Structure: wood／2 stories
Structural engineer:
Masaichi Taguchi (TAPS)

———————

184

澄心寺庫裏
Chushin-ji Temple Priest's Quarters

所在地：長野県上伊那郡箕輪町
用途：寺院庫裏
竣工：2009年
延床面積：226 m²
構造／規模：RC造、木造／地上2階＋ロフト
構造設計者：陶器浩一（滋賀県立大学）、
tmsd 萬田隆構造設計事務所

Location: Minowa-town, Kamiina-district,
Nagano Pref.
Principal use: temple priest's quarters
Completion year: 2009
Total floor area: 226 m²
Structure: reinforced concrete, wood／
2 stories and loft

Structural engineer: Hirokazu Toki
(The University of Shiga Prefecture),
Takashi Manda (tmsd)

———————

194

bird house

所在地：愛知県名古屋市天白区
用途：専用住宅
竣工：2010年
延床面積：134 m²
構造／規模：木造／地上2階
構造設計者：
田口雅一（TAPS建築構造計画事務所）

Location: Tempaku-ku, Nagoya City,
Aichi Pref.
Principal use: residence
Completion year: 2010
Total floor area: 134 m²
Structure: wood／2 stories
Structural engineer:
Masaichi Taguchi (TAPS)

———————

202

elastico

所在地：兵庫県西宮市
用途：美容室
竣工：2010年
延床面積：84 m²
構造：鉄板造

Location: Nishinomiya City, Hyogo Pref.
Principal use: hair salon
Completion year: 2010
Total floor area: 84 m²
Structure: steel plate

———————

210

「元気の種をまく」
Sowing Seeds of Hope

所在地：岩手県釜石市
用途：花壇
実施時期：2011年
（4月上旬頃より構想。7月25日に1回目の
種まき、10月31日に2回目の種まき）
施工面積：61 m²

Location: Kamaishi City, Iwate Pref.
Principal use: flowerbed
Implementation date: 2011
(planning: since the beginning of April,
the first sowing: July 25th,
the second sowing: October 31st)
Construction area: 61 m²

———————

212

宝来館「星めぐりひろば」
'Hoshimeguri Hiroba': Face of
HORAIKAN

所在地：岩手県釜石市
用途：外構および旅館ファサード
竣工：2012年
施工面積：270 m²
構造：RC造、木造
構造設計者：
田口雅一（TAPS建築構造計画事務所）

Location: Kamaishi City, Iwate Pref.
Principal use: exterior, facade of inn
Completion year: 2012
Construction area: 270 m²
Structure: reinforced concrete, wood
Structural engineer:
Masaichi Taguchi (TAPS)

———————

214

真福寺客殿
Shinpuku-ji Temple Reception Hall

所在地：長野県上伊那郡辰野町
用途：寺院客殿
竣工：2013年
延床面積：425 m²
構造／規模：RC造、S造／地上1階
構造設計者：
田口雅一（TAPS建築構造計画事務所）

Location: Tatsuno-town, Kamiina-district,
Nagano Pref.
Principal use: Temple reception hall
Completion year: 2013
Total floor area: 425 m²
Structure: reinforced concrete, steel
frame／1 story
Structural engineer:
Masaichi Taguchi (TAPS)

———————

226

真福寺お通夜部屋増築
Shinpuku-ji Temple Reception Hall
Extension

用途：お通夜部屋
竣工：2014年
延床面積：33 m²
構造／規模：RC造 ／地上1階
構造設計者：
田口雅一（TAPS建築構造計画事務所）

Principal use: funeral vigil room
Completion year: 2014
Total floor area: 33 m²
Structure: reinforced concrete／1 story
Structural engineer:
Masaichi Taguchi (TAPS)

———————

227

真福寺納骨堂内装工事
Shinpuku-ji Temple Ossuary (Renovation)

用途：納骨堂
竣工：2016年
延床面積：9 m²

構造／規模：木造／地上1階
Principal use: ossuary
Completion year: 2016
Total floor area: 9 m²
Structure: wood／1 story

———————

228

tooth

所在地：東京都日野市
用途：歯科医院
竣工：2013年
延床面積：141 m²
構造／規模：RC造、鉄板造、木造／地上2階
構造設計者：
田口雅一（TAPS建築構造計画事務所）

Location: Hino City, Tokyo
Principal use: dental clinic
Completion year: 2013
Total floor area: 141 m²
Structure: reinforced concrete, steel
plate, wood／2 stories
Structural engineer:
Masaichi Taguchi (TAPS)

———————

236

福島第一さかえ原発
Fukushima Dai-ichi Sakae Nuclear Plant

開催地：愛知芸術文化センター
（愛知県名古屋市東区）
用途：インスタレーション
（あいちトリエンナーレ2013）
開催：2013年
展示面積：16,791 m²
テープの総延長：8 km
素材／技法：ラインテープアイロン圧着仕上
げ、カッティングシート、発砲スチロール、コーキ
ング用バックアップ材、合成樹脂塗料

Location: Aichi Arts Center
(Higashi-ku, Nagoya City, Aichi)
Principal use: installation for Aichi
Triennale 2013
Exhibition year: 2013
Exhibition area: 16,791 m²
Total extension of the tape: 8 km
Materials: plastic tape fixed by ironing,
plastic sheet, expanded polystyrene,
sealant backing rod, acrylic resin coating

———————

240

香林寺ファサード改修
Korin-ji Temple Façade Renovation

所在地：東京都八王子市
用途：仏教寺院
竣工：2015年
構造：S造
構造設計者：
田口雅一（TAPS建築構造計画事務所）
Location: Hachioji City, Tokyo
Principal use: temple

Completion year: 2015
Structure: steel frame
Structural engineer:
Masaichi Taguchi (TAPS)

248

香林寺改修 II 期──タカラブネ
Korin-ji Temple Renovation II ──SEVEN GODS' GARDEN

用途：仏教寺院
計画：2015年
延床面積：364 m²
構造／規模：S造／地上2階+ロフト

Principal use: temple
Planning date: 2015
Total floor area: 364 m²
Structure: steel frame／2 stories and loft

250

御船町甘木・玉虫仮設団地 みんなの家
Home-For-All in Amagi and Tamamushi

所在地：熊本県上益城郡御船町
用途：集会所
竣工：2017年
延床面積：各39 m²
構造／規模：木造／地上1階
構造設計者：満田衛資構造計画研究所

Location: Mifune-town,
Kamimashiki-district, Kumamoto Pref.
Principal use: community house
Completion year: 2017
Total floor area: each 39 m²
Structure: wood／1 story
Structural engineer:
Mitsuda Structural Consultants

252

こまめ塾
Komame Commons

所在地：長野県松本市
用途：学習塾、託老所、生協ステーション、
ランドスケープ等
竣工：2019年
延床面積：141 m²
構造／規模：鉄筋による補強CB造の補強／
地上2階
構造設計者：東京大学佐藤淳研究室

Location: Matsumoto City, Nagano Pref.
Principal use: after-school, center for
the aged, consumers' co-op station,
landscape etc.
Completion year: 2019
Total floor area: 141 m²
Structure: reinforcement of concrete
block structure with rebars／2 stories
Structural engineer:
Jun Sato Laboratory, University of Tokyo

260

大阪市立大学工学部 F棟実験室
Osaka City University Faculty of Engineering F Building Laboratories

所在地：大阪府大阪市住吉区
用途：大学実験室
竣工：2020年
延床面積：421 m²（増築部分）
構造／規模：S造／地上1階
共同設計者：上坂設計、YAP（山口陽登）
構造設計者：片岡慎策（片岡構造）、上坂設計

Location: Sumiyoshi-ku, Osaka City,
Osaka Pref.
Principal use: university laboratory
Completion year: 2020
Total floor area: 421 m² (additional area)
Structure: steel frame／1 story
Collaborative architects:
KOSAKA ARCHITECTS INC.,
YAP (Yamaguchi Akito)
Structural engineer:
Kataoka Structural Design Department,
KOSAKA ARCHITECTS INC.

266

上郡町立認定こども園
Kamigori Nursery School

所在地：兵庫県赤穂郡上郡町
用途：認定こども園
竣工：2021年
延床面積：1,398 m²
構造／規模：木造／地上1階
共同設計者：宮本設計
構造設計者：満田衛資構造計画研究所

Location: Kamigori-town, Ako-district,
Hyogo Pref.
Principal use: nursery school
Completion year: 2021
Total floor area: 1,398 m²
Structure: wood／1 story
Collaborative architect:
MIYAMOTO ARCHITECTURAL &
TECHNICAL OFFICE
Structural engineer:
Mitsuda Structural Consultants

272

常泉寺新位牌堂
Josen-ji Temple Tablet Hall

所在地：長野県上伊那郡中川村
用途：寺院位牌堂
竣工：2022年
延床面積：208 m²
構造／規模：木造、RC造、鉄板造／地上1階
構造設計者：tmsd 萬田隆構造設計事務所

Location: Nakagawa-town, Kamiina-
district, Nagano Pref.
Principal use: temple tablet hall
Completion year: 2022

Total floor area: 208 m²
Structure: wood, reinforced concrete,
steel plate／1 story
Structural engineer:
Takashi Manda (tmsd)

280

北九州市立埋蔵文化財センター
（旧八幡市民会館のコンヴァージョン）
Kitakyushu Archaeological Center
(Conversion and Rejuvenation of the former Yahata Civic Hall)

所在地：福岡県北九州市八幡東区
用途：埋蔵文化財センター
竣工：2025年予定
延床面積：約4,884 m²
構造／規模：RC造、一部SRC造／
地下1階、地上3階
共同設計者：東畑建築事務所

Location: Yahatahigashi-ku, Kitakyushu
City, Fukuoka Pref.
Principal use: archaeological center
Completion year: estimated in 2025
Total floor area: 4,884 m²
Structure: reinforced concrete, partly
steel-reinforced concrete／
1 basement and 3 stories
Collaborative architect:
Tohata Architects & Engineers

宮本佳明

1961年兵庫県生まれ。1984年東京大学工学部建築学科卒業。1987年同大学院工学系研究科建築学専攻修士課程修了。博士（工学）。1988年アトリエ第5建築界設立、2002年宮本佳明建築設計事務所に改組。大阪芸術大学助教授、大阪市立大学大学教授などを経て、現在早稲田大学教授。
主な受賞歴に、第6回ヴェネチアビエンナーレ建築展金獅子賞（1996年）、「ゼンカイ」ハウスでJCDデザイン賞ジャン・ヌーベル賞、及び日本建築家協会新人賞（1998年）、「クローバーハウス」で日本建築家協会賞（2007年）、「澄心寺庫裏」で日本建築学会作品選奨（2012年）、建築展「入るかな？はみ出ちゃった。〜宮本佳明 建築団地」で芸術選奨文部科学大臣賞（2024年）。主著に『環境ノイズを読み、風景をつくる。』（彰国社）、『Katsuhiro Miyamoto』（Libria、Italy）、『Katsuhiro MIYAMOTO & Associates』（Nemofactory、Korea）など。

Katsuhiro Miyamoto

Born Hyogo Prefecture in 1961. Graduated in Architecture from the University of Tokyo in 1984. Completed the master program in Architecture at the University of Tokyo in 1987. Ph.D. in Engineering. Established Atelier Cinquiéme Architects in 1988, which was reorganized into Katsuhiro Miyamoto & Associates in 2002. Previously served as an associate professor at Osaka University of Arts and a professor at Osaka City University, currently a professor at Waseda University.
He received the Golden Lion for Best National Participation at the 6th Venice Biennale Architecture Exhibition (1996); Jean Nouvel Award at Japan Commercial Environment Designers Association Design Awards and Young Architect of the Year at Japan Institute of Architects (1998) for *House Surgery*; Japan Institute of Architects Award (2007) for *CLOVER HOUSE*; Annual Architectural Design Commendation 2012 of the Architectural Institute of Japan for *Chushin-ji Temple Priest's Quarters*; the 2024 (74th) Minister of Education's Art Encouragement Prize for *Full Size is oversized: KATSUHIRO MIYAMOTO Architecture Park* (solo exhibition in 2023) and more. Among his main publications are *"Kankyo noizu wo yomi, fuuikei wo tsukuru* (Create Landscape by Reading Environmental Noise Elements)" (Shokokusha, Japan), "Katsuhiro Miyamoto" (Libria, Italy), and "Katsuhiro MIYAMOTO & Associates" (Nemofactory, Korea).

photo credits:

City of Kitakyushu (p.285 menu7_left-top), Kazuo Fukunaga (p.82), Kei Sugino (p.124-127), Ken Oyama (p.81bottom), Kenta Hasegawa (p.260-264top), Koji Kobayashi (p.20bottom, 157bottom), Kunihiko Katsumata (p.228-231, 234), Ryu Namba(p.284 menu3_left-top), Shinkenchiku-sha Co.,Ltd (p.50top, 54-55, 60top, 92-94, 99top, 116-117top, 118-119, 120, 121, 122, 130-133, 138, 144-145, 152-153, 158top, 162-163, 166top, 170-171, 196-197, 200top, 272-277), Takumi Ota (p.25, 36top, 184-189, 192-193, 204-206top, 207, 216-217, 220-223, 226, 227top-left&bottom-left, 240-242, 246top, 254-255, 258, 266-270), Tamio Murakami (p.212-213top), Tetsuo Ito (p.239), Toshio Taira (p.291 menu24_top-right) , Toshihide Kajihara (p.114), Yoshiro Masuda (p.1-11, 14-15, 17-19, 20top, 21, 23, 24, 27-35, 36bottom, 37, 40, 248-249)

Katsuhiro Miyamoto & Associates (the others)

translation:
Leiko Dairokuno（p.282, 284-291／French）

宮本佳明　建築団地

2024年5月27日　初版第一刷発行

著作：宮本佳明

有田泰子＋藤森慧＋原山大＋シア・モリー
［株式会社宮本佳明建築設計事務所］
永井颯馬＋常盤香帆＋澤田一眞
［早稲田大学宮本佳明研究室］

構成・編集・DTP：高木伸成＋小園涼子
［株式会社フリックスタジオ］
デザイン：武田昌也
印刷・製本：藤原印刷株式会社

発行・販売：株式会社フリックスタジオ
〒164-0003
東京都中野区東中野3-16-14 小谷ビル5F
Tel: 03-6908-6671
Fax: 03-6908-6672
E-mail: books@flickstudio.jp［販売部］

KATSUHIRO MIYAMOTO Architecture Park

Produced by Katsuhiro Miyamoto

Yasuko Arita, Kei Fujimori,
Dai Harayama, Sieh Molly
[Katsuhiro Miyamoto & Associates]
Soma Nagai, Kaho Tokiwa,
Kazuma Sawada
[Katsuhiro Miyamoto Laboratory, Waseda University]

Edited by Shinya Takagi, Ryoko Kozono
[flick studio]
Designed by Masaya Takeda
Printed & Bound by
Fujiwara Printing Co., Ltd.

First issued on May 27, 2024

Published by Flick Studio Co., Ltd.
Higashi Nakano 3-16-14-5F,
Nakano-ku, Tokyo, 164-0003
tel: 81-3-6908-6671
fax: 81-3-6908-6672
E-mail: books@flickstudio.jp

ISBN 978-4-904894-61-3